GRAY
MATTER

Speech and Language

GRAY
MATTER

GRAY
MATTER

Speech and Language

Amanda A. Sleeper, Ph.D.

Series Editor
Eric H. Chudler, Ph.D.

CHELSEA HOUSE
P U B L I S H E R S
An imprint of Infobase Publishing

Speech and Language

Chelsea House
An imprint of Infobase Publishing
132 West 31st Street
New York, NY 10001

Library of Congress Cataloging-in-Publication Data

Sleeper, Amanda A.
  Speech and language / Amanda A. Sleeper.
     p. cm.—(Gray matter)
  Includes bibliographical references and index.
  ISBN 0-7910-8952-5 (hardcover)
  1. Speech—Juvenile literature. I. Title.
  QP399.S54 2006

  612.7'8—dc22   2006014261

Chelsea House books are available at special discounts when purchased in bulk quantities for businesses, associations, institutions, or sales promotions. Please call our Special Sales Department in New York at (212) 967-8800 or (800) 322-8755.

You can find Chelsea House on the World Wide Web at
http://www.chelseahouse.com

Series and Cover design by Terry Mallon

Printed in the United States of America

Bang EJB 10 9 8 7 6 5 4 3 2 1

This book is printed on acid-free paper.

All links and Web addresses were checked and verified to be correct at the time of publication. Because of the dynamic nature of the Web, some addresses and links may have changed since publication and may no longer be valid.

Contents

Language:
A Uniquely Human Tool

1

From an infant's first cries at birth, humans begin communicating with one another. As infants grow, they develop a more refined form of communication: language. **Language** uses sounds, symbols, or signs to form words. These words are combined according to rules. This systematic approach allows for an infinite number of ideas to be expressed in a manner understandable to anyone who speaks that language. This rich form of communication is unparalleled in any other species on Earth. Language is a fundamental part of how humans interact with each other and the environment around them (Figure 1.1). We use language to understand and learn about the world. Without language, it might have been impossible for humans to develop an advanced civilization. From artistic expression to scientific progress, language has provided humans with an invaluable tool for sharing our experiences through the millennia and for imparting knowledge across generations. The loss of language ability in injured patients can be devastating, interrupting an individual's capacity to participate in society.

The ability of the brain to develop and coordinate the complexities of language remains a mystery. Scientists are debating how the brain is able to master language. As scientific techniques have become more advanced, scientists are beginning to understand the regions of the brain that participate

Figure 1.1 A young woman talks on a cell phone, which illustrates one of the many ways that we use language to communicate with each other.

in coordinating language. In the past, brain imaging revealed only the brain's structure. New brain imaging techniques, such as **positron emission tomography**, **functional magnetic resonance imaging**, and **magnetoencephalography**, now provide information about the activity of the brain as patients engage in cognitive tasks. As scientists use these tools to better understand how the brain processes language, new opportunities for the treatment of language disabilities will emerge.

This book will discuss the rapid development of language in children, the regions of the brain involved in coordinating speech and language, and the various disorders that disrupt the ability to learn and use language. Spoken language, sign language, and second languages will all be addressed.

2 | Language Development

Children develop language with amazing speed. Language starts out as simple cries and coos, develops into babble, and then progresses to words, phrases, and finally full sentences that increase steadily in grammatical accuracy and complexity. Children learn at their own pace, and some children develop verbal skills more quickly than others. Still, all children pass through the same stages of language ability at one point or another.

Language acquisition begins before a baby starts to talk. Between 0 and 3 months, babies begin to orient to voices. They recognize the familiar voices of their parents and may smile in response. They listen carefully to unfamiliar voices and are comforted by soothing voices, whether the voice is a parent's or an unknown voice. In the second to third month, babies begin to coo, which are soft, wordless vocalizations. Between 4 and 6 months, babies become even more aware of sounds in their environment, including voices, music, the tap of rain on the windows, birds singing, and household noises such as a telephone ring. Usually around 6 months of age, children begin to babble, producing the basic sound elements of a spoken language, called **phonemes**. At this age, babies react when they hear the word "no." By 7 to 12 months, a child's verbal skills begin to develop rapidly. Children begin to realize that people and objects have names, such as "Mommy," "toy," or "nose." Babies become aware of their own names and will look in response when someone calls their name. By one year of age, babies usually speak their first words, typically reflecting the interesting objects in their environment, such as people, animals, or food. They may respond to simple questions or commands, such as "More squash?" or "Give that to Daddy." Between 1 and 2 years of age, children are able to respond to commands such as "Find your blanket." They can successfully point to body parts or point to objects in pictures when they are named. Children begin to delight in hearing simple stories. Their vocabulary steadily grows (Figure 2.1).

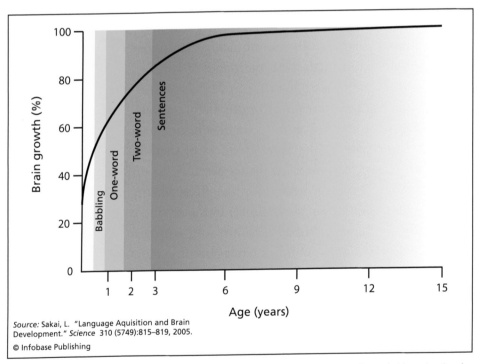

Source: Sakai, L. "Language Aquisition and Brain Development." *Science* 310 (5749):815–819, 2005.
© Infobase Publishing

Figure 2.1 The stages of language development are shown in relation to brain growth. Significant developmental changes in the brain occur during each stage.

By the time children are 2 to 3 years of age, their language skills become more proficient and their ability to form complex sentences increases astronomically. In the first steps, children will make simple word combinations and begin to use two- or three-word phrases: "I got ball," "Big dog," "Eat cracker." Next, they will make requests or ask questions: "What that book doing?" or "Drink a cup a juice." Their grammar is not perfect, but the **syntax** (the word order) of their sentences is usually intact and understandable. Children use both nouns and verbs and understand subjects and objects. As the months pass, their range of grammar becomes more and more complex, their sentences become longer, and they may make their own creative comparisons. For example, they may say, "Let me go out with the hat on," "Derek sounds like a duck," or "How truck be so loud and lift like hands?" Use of verb tense becomes more complex, such as "Grandma coming in 15 minutes," or "I going share that with Amy." During this period, children learn to respond to two-part commands: "Go to your room and get your coat," and form complex sentences of their own. They understand opposites such as "hot" versus "cold" and contrasting prepositions like "in" versus "on." By 3 to 4 years of age, children understand the concepts of who/what/where and, though not always perfectly, can display the full range of grammatical constructions used in adult language. Children also start including function words such as "of," "the," "on," and "does" in their sentences regularly and almost always when required. By 4 to 5 years of age, children rarely make grammatical mistakes and are able to produce language close to adult fluency.

A CRITICAL PERIOD FOR LANGUAGE ACQUISITION

The concept of a **critical period**, a developmental time frame during which a skill is most readily acquired, is an important aspect of language development. If children are deprived of normal, language-based social interactions, they are later unable to master language. One example of such a child is Genie. Genie's parents locked her in a room when she was very young. She spent the first 13 years of her life in isolation. She was rarely spoken to and had interaction with few people. When she was finally found, she had no language skills. She would only utter "No more" and "Stop it," and she did not appear to understand their meaning. Genie was taken to a children's hospital. Her caregivers wondered whether Genie's lack of development was due to isolation, malnutrition, injury, or a true cognitive impairment. They nourished the child and began to teach Genie to take care of herself. She grew healthier, ran, laughed, and learned quickly. She excelled at analyzing patterns and performing spatial-oriented tasks. In one spatial assessment test, Genie was given a set of colored sticks and was asked to re-create from memory a complex structure. She replicated what she had seen perfectly, even using correctly colored sticks in the proper locations. On another test measuring spatial/pattern recognition skills, Genie earned the highest score ever recorded. Clearly, Genie had the ability to learn and showed impressive intelligence.

Genie's language skills, however, did not progress as well as the rest of her learning. Genie discovered some aspects of language quickly. For example, she realized that objects have names. She would ask the names of virtually everything she saw around her and would try to remember them. She learned to form simple, two- to three-word sentences, such as "No want milk," much like the earliest sentences children form. Unlike other children, however, Genie never progressed to form her sentences with correct structure, such as "I don't want any milk." Her ability to communicate verbally stalled at this early stage.

The brain is divided into two hemispheres, a left and a right (Figure 2.2). The brain's language centers are mainly located in the left hemisphere. Spatial processing, in contrast, generally

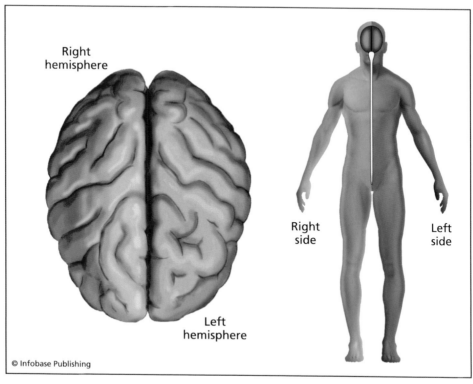

Figure 2.2 The brain is divided into two hemispheres, the left and the right. The left side of the brain controls motor skills of the right side of the body, and the right side of the brain controls the left side of the body. Language centers are mainly housed in the left hemisphere of the brain.

relies on the right hemisphere of the brain. Scientists examined the activity levels in Genie's brain. They were surprised to find that Genie had very little activity in her left hemisphere, but that her right hemisphere was very active. This could be interpreted in various ways. Perhaps Genie suffered damage to the left hemisphere of her brain, leaving her unable to perform language tasks that rely heavily on these regions. She might have been born this way, or it could be a result of many years of neglect, abuse, and malnourishment during important developmental stages. Genie's intact right hemisphere processing argues against general developmental impairment. Alternately, it is possible that Genie was isolated during a critical period of language development, and she had missed the opportunity to fully learn language. Unfortunately, it is difficult for scientists to determine which of these ideas is correct.

A community of deaf individuals has provided additional evidence for the critical period of language acquisition. The country of Nicaragua had no formal education system for the deaf until the mid-1980s. As the country began to develop an education system for the deaf and to teach sign language, educators realized that deaf adults who had grown up in an otherwise normal environment were unable to successfully learn sign language. Deaf young children, however, were more successful, suggesting that their brains were still capable of forming the neural connections necessary for acquiring language.

Additional evidence for a critical period of language acquisition involves a deaf child named Joseph. Joseph was mistakenly diagnosed with cognitive impairments when, actually, he was simply deaf. This was not discovered until Joseph was 11 years old. As a result, he spent the first 10 years of his life without exposure to structured language, though his childhood was otherwise relatively normal. When his deafness was discovered, psychologists tried to teach Joseph sign language, but with limited success. The physician Oliver Sacks described Joseph's abilities in his book *Seeing Voices*:

> Joseph saw, distinguished, categorized, used; he had no problems with perceptual categorization or generalization, but he could not, it seemed, go much beyond this, hold abstract ideas in mind, reflect, play, plan. He seemed completely literal—unable to juggle images or hypotheses or possibilities, unable to enter an imaginative or figurative realm. . . . He seemed, like an animal, or an infant, to be stuck in

the present, to be confined to literal and immediate perception.[1]

This limited language acquisition ability past early childhood is compelling evidence for a critical period of language acquisition. Further, the limited ability of Joseph and others like him to structure ideas and to form plans has led scientists to speculate that language itself is necessary for organized thought.

Scientists are interested in learning why such a critical period for language acquisition exists. One hypothesis is based on the developmental changes that occur in the human brain during the critical period, especially during the time when children in normal environments are rapidly developing their language skills.

EARLY BRAIN DEVELOPMENT

When babies are born, their brains contain nearly all of the **neurons** they will have in a lifetime. In fact, babies have many more neurons than they need. All of the cells are in their proper place. After birth, the brain continues to mature. Neurons make connections with each other, sometimes across long distances. Neuronal connections occur at specialized sites of communication called synapses. Synapses continue to form following birth. The number of synapses in the human brain is at its highest between 9 months and 2 years of age. Often, neurons need to send projections over long distances to make synapses with other neurons. Neurons use electrical activity to send signals across their enormous lengths in order to arrive at distant synapses. To transmit these electrical signals over such long distances reliably, neurons surround their projections with a fatty substance called **myelin** (Figure 2.3).

Myelin helps to insulate the projections and to preserve the electrical signal as it travels. The long-distance connections between neurons are all in place by 9 months of age, but the process of **myelination**, the development of myelin around a nerve fiber, continues to develop through childhood. During childhood, excess neurons that are not active in the brain begin to die off, leaving only successfully communicating neurons behind. The number of synapses between neurons also begins to decline. This pruning continues through adolescence into adulthood. The maturing and refining of the brain early in life parallels the development of language skills,

Imaging the Brain

For centuries, scientists have longed to watch the brain in action. Modern imaging techniques provide glimpses of the brain's responses to stimuli such as tastes, scents, or images. These techniques, including positron emission tomography (PET) and functional magnetic resonance imaging (fMRI), detect increases in blood flow and blood oxygen content that occur in active regions of the brain and are beginning to reveal how the brain controls language.

For PET imaging, patients are injected with a radioactive substance while they lie with their head in a doughnut-shaped scanner. Stimulation leads to activity in the patient's brain, increased blood flow, and a resultant increase in the amount of radioactive material (positrons) in that area. The scanner detects these positrons and creates an image of the brain regions that were activated.

Functional MRI uses a strong magnet to detect changes in the amount of oxygen in the brain's blood. This magnet induces a change in the magnetic field of hydrogen atoms in the brain, which results in the creation of radio signals. These signals are indicating that cellular processes may be required for language development.

Accordingly, by adulthood, when brain structure and connectivity is relatively stable, humans have a difficult time learning new languages, a process that psychologists refer to as **second language acquisition**. Scientists suspect this is because the brain no longer is capable of the dynamic changes that occur during

enhanced when brain activity causes an increase in levels of blood oxygen. This procedure is different from standard MRI, which provides information about anatomy but not about function. Functional MRI is preferred to PET for functional imaging because it provides a sharper image without the use of dangerous radioactive material.

In both PET and fMRI, researchers typically take two types of images: a resting control and a stimulation response. A baseline image is gathered while the patient is resting. Then, stimulation occurs (for example, the patient reads or hears a word). Typically, brain activity is assessed in multiple periods of stimulus exposure or rest. The averaged baseline images are subtracted from the averaged stimulation period images. This remaining image represents the location of activity in one individual's brain that is dependent on the stimulus. Researchers often repeat these experiments with many individuals and average the final images to determine the areas of the brain that are activated by a particular stimulus. Language activates areas of the brain that are distinct from other types of stimulation, such as odor or heat.

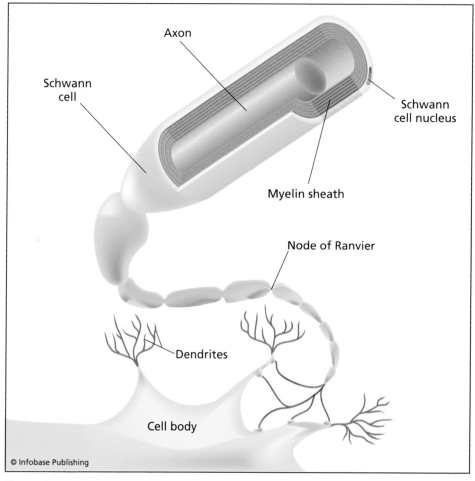

Figure 2.3 A fatty substance called myelin allows neurons to communicate rapidly over long distances. The myelin is provided by Schwann cells, which wrap layers of myelin around the neurons.

childhood's **first language acquisition period**, the development of a native language in young children. Interestingly, though it is more difficult to learn a second language later in life, successful first language acquisition seems to provide a template for additional language acquisition. With work, it is possible for adults to speak a second language fluently.

Though scientists speculate that these biological processes are important for language development, they still don't understand how the brain acquires and processes language. Because of the contrast between the complexities of language and the relative ease by which humans develop language, some scientists believe that the brain has a preexisting structure that predisposes humans to language use. Other scientists believe that, though a sufficiently sophisticated brain is necessary for language, the development of language is primarily due to experience. In the next chapter, we will discuss what is called the nature versus nurture debate regarding language acquisition.

■ **Learn more about language development** Search the Internet for *brain and language, language acquisition,* and *baby babble.*

3 The Nature Versus Nurture Debate of Language

How much of human behavior is learned, and how much are people born with? This question is called the nature versus nurture debate; *nature* refers to skills humans are born with, and *nurture* refers to skills humans learn. No study of language would be complete without a discussion of this ongoing debate regarding language acquisition. Humans are able to learn the intricacies of proper grammar without any formal training. Seemingly effortlessly, children progress from imitating sounds, to learning words, to arranging a potentially infinite number of grammatically organized sentences. By 4 to 5 years of age, they are highly skilled and can form a majority of their sentences properly. In contrast, learning to read and write and learning the rules that govern language are much more difficult skills. Many adults would have a hard time mapping a complex sentence, defining its verb forms, identifying its objects, and so on. Yet these same adults speak fluent and grammatically correct sentences using all of these features. If you were to show these adults an improperly formed sentence, they would most likely be able to identify where the problem is and fix it, even though they might not be able to name the errors that they successfully edited. Without training in linguistics, how is this possible? Considering language from this point of view, it seems a wonder that the human brain is able to efficiently develop its language skills, especially at such an early age.

This mystery of the brain has led some scientists and linguists to propose the idea of a language capacity that exists in the human brain from birth. This is where the nature versus nurture debate begins. The idea of an innate language template in the human brain is controversial. Those who accept this concept are on the "nature" side of the debate. Others believe language abilities are learned by exposure and experience alone without the need for any innate brain attributes beyond its general sophistication. These proponents are on the "nurture" side of the debate.

NATIVISTS AND NON-NATIVISTS

Cognitive scientists have held differing views throughout history regarding the set of abilities humans are born with. The English philosopher John Locke described a newborn infant's mind as a "tabula rasa," a blank slate that is subsequently shaped by sensory experience. At the other extreme is biological determinism, which defines all behavior as innate and predetermined by a person's genetic makeup. Children's growth and development of new abilities is essentially due to the expression of additional genes that had been dormant in the child. Most scientists believe that the reality is probably somewhere in between these two extremes, and they view language ability as a behavior that is genetically based yet also strongly influenced by the environment. The extent of genetic influence is where scientists disagree.

A person does not spontaneously develop language if isolated from language in his environment—neither does a person spontaneously speak languages that he is not exposed to. For instance, a child born in Japan learns to speak Japanese, and not Russian or French, because he is exposed to Japanese in the environment. A Japanese child exposed only to Russian, however, would learn Russian without any greater ease or difficulty than Japanese, in spite of his genetic background. Clearly, some environmental input is necessary for language acquisition. Nevertheless, genetics must be involved, since the way humans use language is unique among all the species. And in contrast to individuals isolated from language, groups of people that are isolated from language may create a language of their own, complete with grammatical rules. For example, prior to Nicaragua's implementation of an educational system for the deaf, communities of deaf individuals existed in which no formal language was taught. Nevertheless, people in these communities had developed their own version of sign language to communicate among themselves. They used a true language that implemented gestures representing specific words. These words were combined according to syntactic rules, just as words are systematically combined in spoken and written language. In this sense, these individuals exemplified an innate capacity for verbal communication, which they developed in the absence of any training whatsoever.

In the 1960s, linguist Noam Chomsky offered an explanation of humans' amazing language acquisition (Figure 3.1). He proposed that the human brain contains a species-specific "language acquisition device" that enables language development. This pre-wiring would allow for language to be acquired in a manner distinct from general learning, facilitating a child's acquisition of language structure from limited samples of language heard in the environment. He and other linguists, psychologists, and scientists, referred to as **nativists**, have provided a compelling amount of evidence supporting this idea. In general, this evidence involves universal aspects of language among all humans, regardless of the language they speak. The non-nativist (or environmentalist) side of the argument sometimes interprets the same evidence in a different way

Figure 3.1 Noam Chomsky gives a speech during a conference in Istanbul, Turkey. Chomsky is an influential figure in the field of linguistics, which is the scientific study of language.

or looks at different evidence that may contradict the nativist view. Whether due to an innate capacity for language or simply due to cultural and environmental norms across societies, the following examples illustrate aspects of language that are common across all cultures.

UNIVERSAL GRAMMAR

All languages contain thousands of words that, theoretically, could be arranged in an infinite number of ways, yet only a subset of these combinations will make comprehensible sentences. For instance, the following sentence is confusing: "Me gave big he book generously yesterday the blue." The problem here is syntax, the ordering of the words in the sentence. Alternate arrangements of these words would create sentences acceptable to an English speaker, and most readers could probably determine a logical meaning of the sentence: "Yesterday, he generously gave me the big, blue book." Alternately, "He generously gave me the big, blue book yesterday."

The following sentence is also confusing, but for different reasons: "The block of wood was torn." The syntax of the sentence is reasonable enough, but the properties of a block of wood don't allow it to be torn. In this case, the sentence is confusing because it presents incompatible concepts. A sentence of the same syntax with a different adjective ("painted" or "carved") would have been acceptable. Thus, the rules of words and grammar allow only a certain subset of word combinations to be used.

Every language has its own set of grammatical rules that must be followed in order to create understandable ideas. The rules vary from language to language. For example, in English, adjectives precede the nouns they modify, while in Spanish, the adjectives most often follow the nouns they modify. Yet in no language can an adjective be used to describe an action. Each language has endings applied to certain words that help to clarify their meaning within a sentence. In English, the ending "ly" is often added to a word to indicate that it is being used as an adverb, to describe an action. If you were able to correctly guess the meaning of the garbled sentence above, you likely used the "ly" ending of the word "generously" as a guide that it must be describing the sentence's only verb, "gave." Furthermore, you may have guessed that "he" was doing the giving, since "me" is always used as an object and not a subject, and in keeping with that line of thought, "he" likely "gave" something to "me." One could have considered the book as the recipient, but as in the sentence with incompatible concepts, generally people don't think of giving items to inanimate objects. It wouldn't make sense to give "me" to "the book" even though this would be an equally acceptable grammatical arrangement. Likewise, it is more likely that the book in the sentence is blue, rather than any of the people. With additional iterations of similar logic, a person can rearrange the sentence into a comprehensible structure. If such a garbled sentence were written in any language, a person would be able to use that language's analogous clues to come up with the same, logical meaning. This exercise illustrates the concept of universal grammar, which can be defined as the structures and functional relationships allowable in human languages.

Studies comparing multiple human languages show consistencies in the logic of sentence formation and in the interpretation of ambiguity, as well as the developmental patterns by which humans learn language. The following are a few examples of seemingly inborn language concepts that could be used to support the idea of an innate language capacity in humans.

Understanding Ambiguity

Chomsky notes that, in addition to the grammatical rules of language, it appears rules also govern the ways humans understand ambiguity. One example Chomsky gives is the phrase "brown house." In any language this phrase is spoken, humans understand grammatical concepts that are not stated directly in the words themselves. For instance, these are two words with two different meanings, and one word describes the other.

Interestingly, in any language such a phrase is delivered, humans universally interpret it to mean that the speaker is talking about a house that is colored brown on the outside, rather than on the inside. Based on the limited information provided in the phrase, it should be logically and grammatically possible for the speaker to mean a house that is brown on the interior, yet it is universally accepted that the color brown refers to the outside of the house. Research shows that even young children, who would not have been taught a rule about this relationship, assume that the speaker must mean a house that is brown on the outside.

Words for Descriptive Concepts

Anthropologist Donald Brown has made observations about the way some descriptive words are used across languages. For example, in English and other languages, the words for "good," "wide," and "deep" have opposites that are distinct words: "bad," "narrow," and "shallow." Other languages create opposites by negating a word, thus "not good," "not wide," or "not deep." However, in no language that creates opposites by negation are the words for "good," "wide," and "deep" expressed as "not bad," "not narrow," or "not shallow." Proponents of the concept of innate language capacity would say that, because this holds true for all languages with opposites formed in this manner, it is as if humans have an innate concept of "good," "wide," and "deep" and incorporate this into speech, contrasting against these properties, rather than the other way around.

Compound Formation

In an effort to determine whether children have an innate sense of linguistic rules, in 1985, psychologist Peter Gordon of the University of Pittsburgh studied a rule used in the English language: compounding. Gordon was interested in the way humans link two words to describe a trait. An example would be the term "dog-lover." If a man is described to really love dogs, he could be termed a "dog-lover." Although he loves all dogs and not just one particular dog, the English language does not permit the man to be termed a "dogs-lover," and when the term "dog-lover" is used, English speakers understand the compound to refer to someone who loves dogs in general rather than one specific dog, even though the singular form of the word "dog" is used. To determine if this rule of compounding is learned or innate, Gordon studied the rule in children between the ages of 3 and 5 years, an age at which children are unlikely to have heard much compounding in speech and when they do not naturally form compounds on their own. He showed the children a puppet and told them that the puppet liked to eat mud. Since the puppet liked to eat mud, he would call the puppet a mud-eater. He went through a variety of singular nouns using the -eater example to familiarize the children with the compound formation. Then he asked them to decide what to call the puppet under different circumstances. When the puppet was described to enjoy eating a rat, the children called the puppet a "rat-eater." If the puppet liked to eat mice, the children called him a "mice-eater" or a "mouse-eater," and if he liked to eat rats (a key plural word ending in "s"), the children correctly termed the puppet a "rat-eater" rather than a "rats-eater." Even children who used the incorrect term "mouses" in their speech never called a puppet that likes to eat a mouse or mice a "mouses-eater." This evidence suggests that certain language paradigms (in this case not using a plural form ending in "s" to create a compound word) are innate rather than learned.

UNIVERSAL DEVELOPMENT OF LANGUAGE

In addition to the seemingly universal grammar that exists across all languages, predictable developmental stages of language acquisition also exist. No matter what language a child is learning, development usually occurs within a particular time frame. Furthermore, during the stages of language acquisition, predictable mistakes occur. One would expect greater variation to exist if there were no predetermined language acquisition mechanism in the brain. For example, many humans typically learn only the one language that they are exposed to during childhood. When people learn a second language later in life, this is the result of concentrated study, rather than the seemingly automatic process that occurs during the first language acquisition of childhood. In contrast to first language acquisition, second language acquisition does not occur along a predictable timeline. There is great variability among individuals, further emphasizing the amazing regularity with which children acquire their first language.

Babbling

When children begin to babble, their first strides toward speech, they produce all sorts of sounds, including the phonemes that comprise their native language as well as those that are used in other languages but not in the speech heard around them. Children produce these sounds without being taught (otherwise they would form only those sounds unique to the language they hear). Children stop producing sounds extraneous to their native language only after they learn the constraints of their own language. This tendency to form vocalizations used in all languages shows that the brain has a preset ability to form the many sounds that can potentially be used in spoken language.

Overgeneralization

As children gradually acquire more complex language abilities, they tend to overgeneralize rules. An example of this in the English language is the way in which children apply the ending "ed" to describe an action that occurred in the past. Children begin to use this form for verbs such as "walk," as in "We walked outside." They additionally apply this form to irregular verbs, as in "Jeff breaked my toy." If children acquired language solely by imitation, one would not expect these errors of overgeneralization, since adults do not use these forms in their speech. The child would instead use the proper form, "Jeff broke my toy." Yet even when parents try to correct these grammatical errors, children will persist with their own form:

Child: Jeff breaked my toy.
Parent: You mean Jeff broke your toy?
Child: Yes, he breaked my toy!

Analogous errors occur in all languages as children learn the grammatical elements that provide additional meaning to words. These predictable stages of verbal development observed across many languages have been viewed as evidence that all humans gradually acquire their language's grammar in universal, preset, developmental stages that are a result of human brain structure and function.

Ability to Form Creative and Unique Ideas

As children progress in their use of language, the ideas they express become increasingly complex, moving from the concrete ("What that doggy doing?") to the abstract. For instance, children learn to use creative similes and metaphors based on concepts that they have learned. A child who has learned the meaning of "dizzy" and the meaning of "tornado" may make his own unique pairing of the concepts and exclaim while he is playing and becomes dizzy, "I feel like there is a tornado in my head!" At predictable ages, when children understand more complex language, they enjoy hearing stories and eventually telling stories of their own (true or imagined). They move from using language to express ideas about the here and now and begin to connect strings of sentences to express complicated series of events or abstract interpretations. If language were wholly learned by imitation, it would be improbable that children would learn so quickly (if at all) to make unique word combinations. Another abstraction that children quickly develop is the use of **metalinguistics**. Metalinguistics refers to the use of language to discuss language itself (thus the majority of this text is metalinguistic). Children ask questions, such as "How do you say this word?" or "What do you call this?" They begin to use language to think about language and to think about thought itself.

Many would argue that these examples support the concept of an innate language capacity. The universality of language suggests a programmed capacity in the brain that guides how language is used in relation to our senses. Further, maturation of the brain's predefined mechanisms could explain the rapid and predictable stages of language acquisition. If language were not preprogrammed, one might expect slower and more variable language acquisition in children.

The non-nativists, however, look at this same information yet conclude that human language can be explained in the same way that other human behaviors are understood. Just as language has predictable stages of development, so does motor coordination. As the brain and the body mature, coordination improves. This is true of humans and other animals alike. The same developmental processes that underlie coordination could also underlie language acquisition and might provide insight into why all humans progress at about the same pace—it simply takes that amount of time for the brain to mature.

While nativists believe that gradually increased brain sophistication over generations paved the way for language ability, non-nativists would argue something different, that the development of language allowed an already complex brain to finally realize its potential. Non-nativists suggest that universal trends in language use could perhaps be due to cultural standards that have been passed down from generation to generation, rather than an innate, genetically predetermined usage. Nativists have explained the uniquely human aspects of language with genetic evolution. These changes would occur very slowly, over thousands and thousands of years. Yet cultural concepts can be passed very rapidly. Some archaeological evidence supports the idea that language developed in the absence of gradual changes in brain structure. Archaeologists believe that the human brain's shape and size were developed thousands of years prior to thoroughly modern behavior, including symbolic thought and, along with it, structured language. These advances seem to have developed in a sudden explosion of progress, rather than in small, genetically mediated steps.

As of now, however, the mechanisms underlying the astounding process of human language acquisition are still hypothetical, with limited experimental strategies in place to test these ideas. If scientists begin to unravel how language acquisition occurs, this will provide fascinating information about how the brain works. The language acquisition device that Chomsky proposed is not considered a literal device within the human brain that can be isolated. It is considered to be more of a framework by which the human brain organizes language-related stimuli observed in the environment, allowing for the rapid development of language skills that humans can subsequently use to express an infinite possibility of ideas. That said, however, research has shown that particular regions of the brain are, in fact, involved in processing specific aspects of speech and language (including areas that govern grammar) in all humans, regardless of their native language. Scientists have worked to identify these regions, their contributions to language, and the ways in which they cooperate in hopes of better understanding how the brain processes language.

4 Language Centers of the Human Brain

Scientists have only a limited understanding of how the brain regulates the complexities of language. Historically, scientists have gleaned information about the brain areas involved in speech and language by correlating deficits in these behaviors with specific brain injuries. For example, if a person had an injury that damaged part of the brain, and after that injury the person was unable to remember new facts, then one could conclude that the damaged region controls memory consolidation. As modern technologies have provided new ways of examining the brains of normal, conscious individuals, scientists have been able to expand their knowledge of the language centers of the human brain.

The brain contains billions of neurons, which are cells that process sensory information coming in from the environment and coordinate the body to react to its environment. Perception of and response to the environment requires many neurons to signal information to each other in rapid sequence. Groups of neurons that receive sensory information send messages to adjacent neurons, which in turn communicate with additional neurons until the information is processed and a response is executed. Distinct actions and behaviors are coordinated by subsets of the brain's neurons communicating with each other. These subsets are often referred to as neuronal circuits.

Neurons have complicated structures, including axons, dendrites, and cell bodies, that allow signals to travel rapidly into the brain and back out to the body. Neurons communicate with each other through their **axons**, which are long fibers that sometimes travel great distances before reaching their targets. Electrical signals travel down an axon and cause the neuron to release **neurotransmitters** (the signaling chemicals of the brain) to the next neuron in a circuit. The **synapse** is the point where the two neurons meet. **Dendrites** form extensive branches off of a neuron's cell body and receive neurotransmitters released into the synapse. This information can be excitatory (promoting electrical signals to travel through the dendrites, into the cell body, and down the axon to relay information to the next cell) or inhibitory (decreasing the likelihood that an electrical signal will be generated). The cell body of a neuron is where the inputs and outputs of a neuron are coordinated. Scientists are interested in learning the subsets of neurons involved in behaviors and how they work together. They are beginning to understand the regions within the human brain whose neurons are important for governing speech and language.

The **cerebral cortex** is the outermost region of the brain and is important for higher functioning. It comprises 85% of the human brain's total mass and houses the brain's most advanced language centers.[2] A structure called the corpus callosum is a thick band of fibers that connects the left and right sides of the cerebral cortex. The surface of each hemisphere can be divided into four major lobes: the **frontal lobe**, the **temporal lobe**, the **parietal lobe**, and the **occipital lobe** (Figure 4.1). Different cognitive functions typically utilize one side of the brain preferentially over the other side. Research shows that the brain relies primarily on specialized regions of the left hemisphere for processing language.

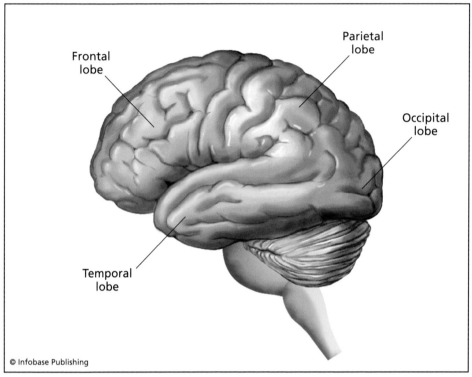

Figure 4.1 Each hemisphere of the brain is divided into four lobes.

LOCALIZATION OF BRAIN FUNCTION

As we have noted, the study of the brain's control of speech and language has historically focused on individuals with impairments, since there was no technology to effectively study brain activity in the normal population. The ancient Greeks noted that damage to the brain could result in a disruption of the ability to form speech. By the nineteenth century, it was widely accepted that the brain is responsible for controlling thought and behavior, and students of the brain theorized that discreet locations within the brain were responsible for carrying out specific aspects of behavior. In 1836, the researcher

Marc Dax described in his memoirs a correlation between left hemisphere damage and loss of speech after having observed this trend in more than 40 of his patients. In 1861, a French neurologist, Paul Broca, published a case study that supported this concept of localization. Broca identified a brain region in the left frontal lobe of the brain that is critical for speech production. This area is now called **Broca's area**. Years later, a German physician, Karl Wernicke, described a second brain region involved in a separate aspect of speech and language: comprehension. This area, a region of the brain located in the temporal lobe, is now called **Wernicke's area**. Since these findings, scientists have accepted that Broca's area is necessary for speech production and that Wernicke's area is necessary for speech comprehension.

Broca's Area

Paul Broca published a case study that described a patient who had lost the ability to form speech. Though the patient was able to understand language spoken to him, if asked a question, the patient replied with just one syllable repeated over and over: "tan." In the hospital, the patient eventually became known as Tan. After Tan died, Broca performed an autopsy of his brain and found damage to an area in the left frontal lobe of the cortex. In his case study, Broca hypothesized that this region of the brain is responsible for the production of speech. This was the first publication providing evidence to link a specific brain region to a cognitive function and to offer proof of the theories of brain localization.

Modern brain imaging research has revealed that Broca's area contributes to other aspects of language in addition to speech production (Figure 4.2). The central portion of Broca's area governs articulation of speech, while the upper portion of this region contributes to comprehension of the meaning of words.

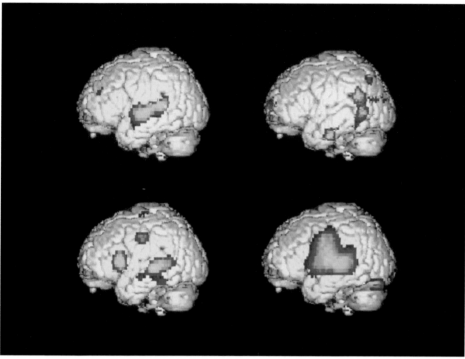

Figure 4.2 This PET (positron emission tomography) scan shows the brain areas that are active while speaking and listening. In the bottom left scan, Wernicke's area is active *(right)*, as is Broca's area *(left)* and part of the motor cortex *(middle)*.

Broca's area is highly active when people are asked to remember a list of words.

Wernicke's Area

Karl Wernicke described two patients who, though able to speak, were unable to form coherent speech and were also unable to understand language spoken to them. After these patients died, Wernicke examined their brains and found that the patients both suffered similar brain damage in an area now labeled Wernicke's area. This region is further back and lower in the brain than Broca's area, in the left temporal lobe adjacent to the parietal lobe.

Modern imaging studies have further revealed how Wernicke's area contributes to language. It is important for both comprehension of incoming language, whether spoken words, written words, or sign language. It is also crucial for proper formation of outgoing speech. When subjects are working on object identification tasks, their brains utilize Wernicke's area in conjunction with Broca's area.

Confirming Left Hemisphere Dominance

In the 1950s, two brain surgeons, Wilder Penfield and Herbert Jasper, performed brain stimulation experiments on consenting patients and confirmed the correlation observed between language and the left hemisphere of the brain, which houses Broca's area and Wernicke's area. During brain surgery, it is often customary to use local anesthesia only, so the patients are fully conscious during the procedure and able to communicate. The surgeons reasoned that they could therefore assess the effects of electrical stimulation of regions of the brain on the patients' ability to communicate verbally. During the surgeries, the doctors asked the patients questions. When the left hemisphere was stimulated, the patients' ability to speak was disrupted, and they were unable to respond to the questions. When the right hemisphere was stimulated, however, the patients were able to successfully answer all of the questions the doctors asked them.

The **Wada test**, a procedure developed in the 1960s, further confirmed the role of the left hemisphere in speech and language. During this test, an anesthetic called sodium amytal is injected into either the left carotid artery (which supplies blood to the left hemisphere of the brain) or the right carotid artery (which supplies the right side of the brain). The anesthetic effectively puts one half of the brain to sleep after it is injected. If the anesthetic is injected into the right hemisphere and the subject is then asked a question, the subject has no problem giving an answer, but if the anesthetic is injected into the left hemisphere, the subject is unable to make replies.

CHALLENGES TO THE CONCEPT OF LOCALIZATION

Language is a complex human behavior. Although Broca's area and Wernicke's area are indeed critical for language, additional neocortical and subcortical areas are also involved in the generation and processing of speech and language. Modern imaging techniques have helped to identify the following neocortical areas: the auditory, motor, and visual cortices, the angular gyrus, and the tracts that interconnect them. Though it may be

Phrenology

Franz Joseph Gall was a nineteenth-century physician from Vienna, Austria. He correctly believed that the brain is responsible for establishing a person's intellect and personality. He was a proponent of the idea that the brain contains discreet locations that govern each aspect of intellect and personality and that these locations are the same in all individuals. This concept of localization set the stage for the important work of physicians such as Broca and Wernicke, whose findings contribute to our knowledge of the brain today. Gall, though, hypothesized that the prominence of a person's traits and skills is a result of the size of brain matter a person has in each specialized region. He also hypothesized that the size and shape of the brain determines the size and shape of a person's skull, and therefore reasoned that the shape of the skull serves as an indicator of a person's character and intellectual aptitude. He called these beliefs phrenology. Gall went on to study the skulls of many patients, looking for prominent skull shapes and correlating them with the patients' personalities and intellectual argued that each of these areas provides a discreet contribution to speech and language, the overall production and comprehension of speech and language requires these areas, and the millions of neurons within them, to work in cooperation. In this sense, language could be considered a global function of the brain (Figure 4.3).

It would be impossible to produce speech without appropriate control of the muscles involved in speech generation. In the frontal lobe, regions called the **motor cortex** and the **motor association cortex** contribute to speech production. The motor cortex allows for the initiation of all of our voluntary muscle

strengths. He then mapped where he believed each trait could be represented on the skull.

Through the nineteenth century, Gall's ideas gained popularity across Europe and in America. Phrenologists would run their fingertips over the heads of their subjects to feel the bumps and indentations of the skull, or they would use calipers to precisely measure the skull's shape. The phrenologist would then offer insights into the intellect of the subject. Employers would hire phrenologists to screen potential employees, ensuring that they would be honest and hardworking. Eventually, phrenology became a part of popular culture in the way that astrology is today. Phrenologists were called upon to provide career advice to young men and to help people determine suitable mates. The popularity of phrenology as an insight into the human mind persisted well into the late nineteenth century, in spite of a lack of concrete evidence that there was any scientific merit behind its tenets.

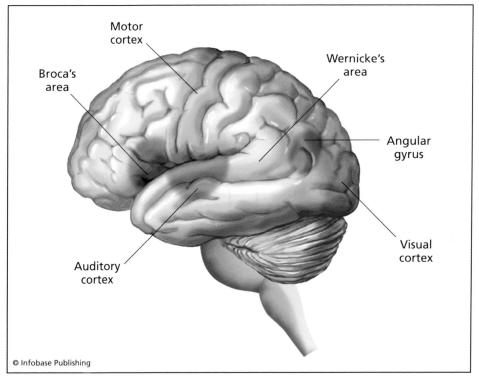

Figure 4.3 Many different regions of the brain are critical for speech and language.

movements. The motor association cortex coordinates movements, including lip movements required for speech.

Auditory and visual regions of the brain are also important for speech and language. The **auditory cortex** and the **auditory association cortex,** both located in the temporal lobe, allow humans to interpret the sounds that they hear. The auditory cortex is the general area where the processing of sound quality occurs. The auditory association cortex more specifically is involved in interpreting complex auditory stimuli and in making sense of sounds. Humans rely on these areas to perceive language spoken by others and to provide feedback about their own voices as they are forming their own speech. If a person loses the ability to hear, his speech clarity deteriorates due to a lack of information from auditory areas of the brain. In addition to auditory regions, the **visual cortex**, in the occipital lobe of the brain, is also involved in speech and language. This region is necessary for reading and writing language. It is also activated as the first step in naming objects, in which a visual image of an object is linked with the word that represents it.

Another cortical area involved in language is the **angular gyrus**, which lies on the edge of the parietal lobe, adjacent to the temporal lobe, about halfway between Wernicke's area and the visual cortex. Many different types of neurons send their axons through this area, including axons carrying information about hearing, vision, and meaning. The angular gyrus is responsible for recognition of visual symbols, such as the letters and punctuation marks on this page. This area, in addition to the visual cortex, is also necessary for reading and writing language. As with Broca's area and Wernicke's area, this area was first linked to language because a patient with a deficit in reading and writing was later discovered to have damage to this region of his brain.

All of the areas of the cortex involved in speech and language are interconnected, which enables the brain to efficiently process language. Some of this circuitry is known. Broca's area and Wernicke's area are interconnected by a bundle of fibers called the **arcuate fasciculus**. This tract is important for the relay of information between these areas. This tract also connects into the angular gyrus. As with damage to Broca's area and Wernicke's area, damage to the arcuate fasciculus results in language deficits. When this connecting region suffers damage, patients are still able to understand language and, with effort, are able to speak, but they are unable to repeat words that they have heard spoken to them.

Variability Among Individuals

Scientists have pinpointed locations within the language areas of the brain that are responsible for precise functions, such as naming vegetables or tools. As with Broca's area and Wernicke's area, these areas were identified by correlating damaged regions of the brain with specific functions based on individuals with injury-induced language deficits. What is surprising is that these areas are not the same in all individuals. Two individuals with the same lesion may have distinct deficits, and two patients with the same deficit may turn out to have different lesions. Even some of the most general findings about localization of speech and language regions do not hold true for some individuals. For example, though the majority of people process speech and language in the left hemisphere of the brain, imaging studies have shown that some individuals with normal language abilities process speech and language with the right hemisphere. Gender studies have revealed that women tend to use additional regions of the right hemisphere when processing language, while men tend to rely on the left hemisphere predominantly.

Recent research suggests that different regions of the brain may be used for the same general function, depending on subtleties in the stimulus. For example, researchers in England found that men utilized two distinct areas of the brain when identifying the gender of human speech. Men identify female voices, which are characterized by higher variability in pitch and intonation (melodic quality) than male voices, in a region of the right hemisphere that is used to analyze complex music. In contrast, the men's brains activated a region called the precuneus, located in the parietal lobe near the midline of the brain, when identifying other male voices. This region is responsible for retrieving episodic memories and for imagining sounds. As of yet, no studies have determined whether females also process male and female voices with different regions of their brains.

One Function Dependent on Two Areas

Another challenge to the concept of localization of speech and language is illustrated by language comprehension. As we have discussed, scientists are confident that Wernicke's area is necessary for language comprehension. Broca's area, however, also appears to contribute to the comprehension of complex aspects of grammar. Patients with damage to Broca's area tend to misunderstand sentences formed in the passive tense. For example, a patient would understand the sentence "The student was corrected by her teacher" to mean that the student was doing the correcting. The brain most likely processes language comprehension with multiple language centers, rather than just Wernicke's area, as previously thought.

Plasticity of the Brain's Language Areas

Plasticity of the brain refers to its ability to adapt by forming new connections. The plasticity of the brain's language areas offers yet another challenge to the concept of localization. Following injury, the brain is sometimes able to compensate for the damaged area by shifting the affected functions to a new location of control. This is especially true when the damage occurs at a young age, which is when the brain shows its greatest plasticity. For example, if the left hemisphere is damaged, a patient may go on to develop normal speech, but analysis shows that language processing in this individual is localized in the right hemisphere to a greater extent than in other humans. Another example of plasticity in language centers has been observed in people who have lost their vision and learned to read using Braille. Brain imaging studies of these people, when they are reading Braille, show that both visual and touch-related centers of the brain are involved during the reading task, while in sighted individuals reading text from a page, only visual centers are activated. The brains of the blind

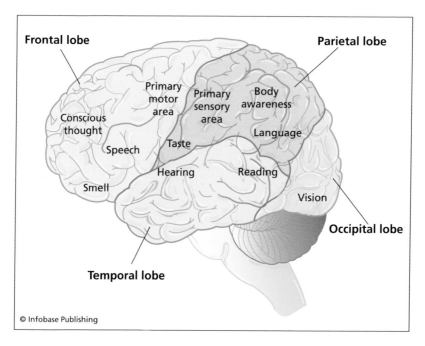

Figure 4.4 In addition to regions for speech and language, the brain can be mapped to show where various other functions reside.

subjects learned to compensate for the loss of sight by utilizing new cells in order to learn language in a new format.

Speech and language are sophisticated functions that utilize specialized regions of the human cortex (Figure 4.4). Imaging studies show these areas as discreet regions of the brain, and damage to any one of these areas can lead to language deficits. Nevertheless, language is a global function, requiring cooperation among the neurons of these areas for successful comprehension and expression. Though scientists have identified key regions involved in language and have begun to determine their contributions to language, these findings are only the first steps in understanding the intricacies of the brain's ability to process language. Future research will begin to unravel the cellular mechanisms that drive this uniquely human behavior.

■ **Learn more about language centers of the brain** Search the Internet for *Wernicke's area*, *Broca's area*, and *Wada test*.

5 Subcortical Regions Involved in Speech Production

In the last chapter, we discussed how information is processed in the **neocortex**, which is the top layer of the cerebral hemispheres. In addition to the cortical regions necessary for processing human language, additional subcortical brain structures contribute to language by receiving and relaying incoming information and by coordinating signals necessary for the production of speech. Scientists have learned much of what is known about these portions of human language centers by the use of animal models.

ANIMAL MODELS

Some animals can learn limited meaning of words spoken to them. For instance, a dog can learn the meaning of the word "sit" and can respond appropriately. Nevertheless, the dog does not have the ability to form such language on its own, and the dog's scope of language comprehension is vastly limited compared to that of humans. The dog uses limited vocalizations (barks, growls, and whimpers) to communicate basic things such as aggression or discomfort. In comparison, human language is unique in its capacity for representation of concrete objects and actions as well as abstract concepts.

Scientists typically rely on animal models to study the cellular mechanisms that drive behaviors or underlie diseases. If a behavior is sufficiently similar between animals and humans, often the processing that goes on in the animal brain is similar to that of the human brain. Because human language is so complex, there are no animal models available for comparison. Some aspects of speech formation, however, are analogous to the vocalization process of other animals, even though the vocalizations of animals lack the complexity of human language. By studying the neural systems supporting vocalizations of other species, scientists have learned how some of the basic mechanisms of human speech production are coordinated.

The human brain deals with language in a hierarchical manner. Some of the most basic functions of language, such as the breathing and muscle control necessary for vocalization, occur similarly in humans and many other species. As properties of language become more complex, the behaviors are further coordinated by additional, specialized regions of the brain present only in those species capable of vocalization at that level of complexity. Neocortical regions with no clear animal counterpart, such as those described in Chapter 4, govern the most complex aspects of human language.

The complexity of the neural systems recruited for vocalization in a given species' brain parallels the sophistication of the species' vocalizations. Most animals are born able to produce all of the vocalizations unique to their species, including dogs, cats, most birds, and non-human primates. Even though these animals need to learn to associate each sound with an appropriate meaning (for example, a predatory alarm versus a mating call), there is no learning necessary for them to be able to produce these sounds. These animals can be called non-learners with respect to vocalization. Non-learners utilize the simplest schema for speech production. Other species produce more varied vocalizations and need to learn to produce these sounds by hearing and mimicking them. These "learners" include limited groups of birds (parrots, hummingbirds, and some songbirds) and mammals (humans, bats, and cetaceans such as whales and dolphins). The brain regions utilized by non-learners are also utilized by these species, but additional, more specialized brain areas are also required. When humans perform language tasks, they are likely to employ regions of the brain that are analogous to those of non-learners and learners, as well as the additional language regions that are unique to humans. By studying the vocalization circuitry of animals with relatively complex, learned vocalizations, scientists have begun to better understand the areas involved in human speech production. Though these studies can't explain all of the circuitry involved in human language, they provide us with information about some of the human language mechanism that we would otherwise be unable to study due to the invasiveness of the techniques.

PRODUCTION OF VOCALIZATION

The most basic aspect of language is the production of vocalization. To form vocalizations, the brain must regulate respiration and the muscles of the larynx (the area of the throat containing the vocal cords) and the mouth. Regions within the lowest portion of the brain, called the **brain stem**, control these functions (Figure 5.1). The brain stem rests just above the spinal cord and links the **peripheral nervous system** to higher regions of the brain. This region is responsible for functions necessary for survival, such as respiration, heart rate, blood pressure, and digestion. Extending from the brain stem is a group of nerves called the **cranial nerves**. Among other functions, the cranial nerves control the muscles of the vocal system. Also in this region of the brain lays a bundle of neurons called the **nucleus ambiguous**. The motor neurons of the nucleus ambiguous help to regulate respiration. Cells within the **medulla oblongata**, a subsection of the brain stem, serve to coordinate the muscles that participate

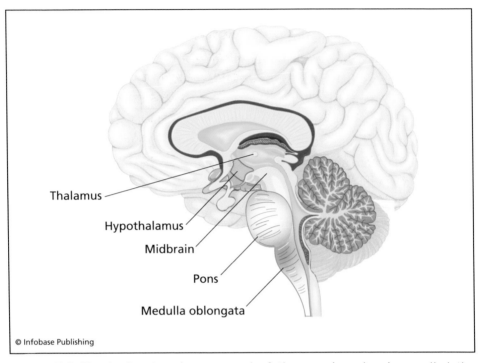

Thalamus

Hypothalamus

Midbrain

Pons

Medulla oblongata

© Infobase Publishing

Figure 5.1 The brain stem is composed of three main subregions called the medulla oblongata, pons, and midbrain. Nerves originating in the midbrain, called the cranial nerves, are essential for speech and the production of sound. Cells in a region called the nucleus ambiguous help to control breathing that is necessary for vocalization. Regions of the medulla oblongata coordinate the activity of the brain stem.

in respiration and vocalization. All animals, whether their vocalizations are simple or complex, utilize brain regions analogous to these to produce their vocalizations.

In species with complex vocalizations, additional regions of the brain stem, as well as higher brain areas, are involved in vocalization. The **midbrain** is a subdivision of the brain stem. Within the midbrain are two regions called the **periaqueductal gray (PAG)** and the **parabrachial tegmentum**. Scientists have determined that activity in these regions is necessary for production of full vocal patterns in animals with complex vocalizations. If these regions of the brain are electrically stimulated, animals will produce full vocal patterns. In contrast, when the lower speech areas that are common with non-learners are stimulated, only fragments of vocalizations are produced.

The limbic system lies just beneath the neocortex and wraps around the brain stem. It is important, in general, for emotion, learning, and memory, though portions of the limbic system also participate in complex vocalization. A region of the limbic system called the **cingulate gyrus** helps initiate vocalization. This region is connected to the PAG region of the brain stem. Like the PAG, when this region of the brain is electrically stimulated, it causes an animal to produce its full vocal patterns. A condition called akinetic mutism occurs when this region is damaged in the human brain. These patients become mute following their injuries.

Additional subcortical areas are involved in production of complex vocalization in animals that are learners. Because of the learning component of these vocalizations, they are more sophisticated than complex vocalizations of non-learners and draw on additional brain regions for coordination. In humans, these areas are part of the largest region of the brain, called the forebrain, and include the subcortical regions called the **thalamus** and **basal ganglia,** which form a connective loop with additional regions of the forebrain. This loop is necessary for vocal learning. Non-human vocal learners, such as songbirds, have brain regions analogous to the basal ganglia and thalamus. Based on the known function of these regions in the vocalizations of animals, scientists have hypothesized aspects of language that they regulate in humans. These functions include fluency, volume, articulation, and rhythm of speech.

The thalamus acts as an important relay center in the brain. Located centrally, it is interconnected with the brain stem, the

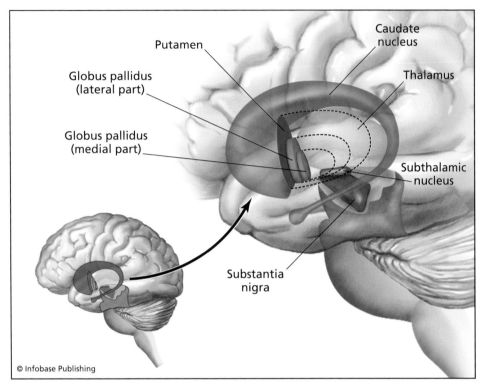

Figure 5.2 The basal ganglia consist of a number of different clusters of neurons. Damage to the basal ganglia can result in speech or language defects.

limbic system, and the neocortex, all of which contribute to regulation of speech and language. The thalamus sends incoming sensory information (touch, sound, and visual information) to the appropriate regions for processing and conducts signals from the cortex through the lower regions of the brain and out to the body. Not only does the thalamus direct signals throughout the brain, it also is able to modulate these signals. The thalamus is important for motor control of the body.

The basal ganglia are a collection of nuclei (clusters of neurons with related function) located at the base of the cerebral hemispheres (Figure 5.2). Together, the cells of the basal ganglia contribute to the regulation and coordination of movement. In humans, the basal ganglia's circuit with the thalamus may serve to refine the ordering of vocal movements necessary for fluent and expressive speech. In young songbirds, damage to the circuitry between the thalamus, basal ganglia, and cortex disrupts vocal learning, and these birds have disordered song sequences that they never learn to correct. Songbirds produce variations in their vocalizations depending on whether they are singing alone or in the presence of other birds. Damage to this circuit in adult songbirds disrupts distinctions in songs that are dependent on such social conditions. Limited information is available on the contribution of this circuitry to human language, but damage in this region can disrupt proper articulation of language as well as some language comprehension. Children who have severe language learning impairments often have an abnormally small volume of the **caudate nucleus**, one of the nuclei of the basal ganglia. This correlation suggests that the caudate nucleus contributes to humans' ability to learn language. Recent brain imaging studies suggest that humans rely on activity in this region when speaking in a second language, though they don't use this area as much when speaking in their native language, which is a more automatic process in the brain.

The **cerebellum** is another region of the brain important for learning motor tasks. There is evidence that this structure further coordinates the motor activities necessary for human vocalization. The cerebellum is especially active during learning periods for language, though it seems to contribute less to speech after language has been learned. Once vocal patterns have been acquired, the cerebellum is important for establishing the rate and rhythm of speech. People with damage to the cerebellum may have trouble with speech that requires practice and may have trouble detecting errors in speech.

What the Zebra Finch Can Teach Us About Speech

Scientists are studying the vocalization mechanisms of animals that are vocal learners, meaning they acquire their repertoire of sounds through mimicry of adults. One such vocal learner is a songbird called the zebra finch. The songs of individual zebra finches are unique, just like human voices and fingerprints. In order to learn appropriate vocalization patterns, zebra finches must be exposed to the songs of other zebra finches by 65 days of age, and they must practice their own songs by the time they reach 90 days of age. If the songbirds miss this critical period of learning, they will never learn how to sing properly. Scientists have characterized two distinct neural circuits in the zebra finch brain governing song. One is responsible for vocal learning, and the other for vocalization subsequent to the learning period. This vocal circuitry has parallels in the human brain. Because both zebra finches and humans must learn their songs and speech, respectively, scientists are using the zebra finch as a model to investigate how humans learn language. They hope to uncover some of the mechanism that underlies learning and memory.

Scientists have found that a small number of zebra finches exhibit irregularities in their song patterns. These irregularities are characterized by repetition of single notes within a song, occurring at regular frequencies. The consistent frequency of these repetitions has led researchers to believe that the repetitions are involuntary, much like stuttering in humans. Scientists are in the process of characterizing this "stuttering" behavior in zebra finches and hope to determine its neural basis. This valuable information may provide clues to the causes of stuttering in humans.

A RELAY OF INFORMATION THROUGH THE BRAIN

Brain imaging studies have shown a relay of brain activity among the regions involved in language when individuals perform language-based activities. These studies reveal how the various regions of the brain involved in speech and language processing work in cooperation. For example, when subjects speak a written word, the first part of the brain to become active is the visual cortex, which the subject uses to process the visual information encoded by the written word. Next, information is sent to Wernicke's area where comprehension of the visual stimulus occurs. Then information is relayed through the arcuate fasciculus to Broca's area, to generate speech production. Broca's area is necessary to direct the neurons of the motor cortex to control the lips and speech muscles necessary for producing the word that was read. Broca's area is located near the region of the motor cortex controlling the mouth, allowing for efficient transmission of information from one area to the other. The information gathered from animal studies suggests that, following activation of the motor cortex, this motor signal is then relayed through the lower language centers of the brain and eventually promotes vocalization of the word that was read. A slightly different relay occurs when patients repeat a word that they have heard. First, the auditory cortex is activated, which then sends a message to Wernicke's area. Then the relay continues to Broca's area and on to the motor cortex. From the motor cortex, the relay continues to produce vocalization, as it does when the word was read.

■ **Learn more about subcortical regions involved in speech** Search the Internet for *basal ganglia* and *brain and speech.*

6 Sign Language and Second Languages

It is all too easy to take language, one's own language, for granted—one may need to encounter another language, or another mode of language, in order to be astonished, to be pushed into wonder, again.

Oliver Sacks[3]

Sign language is a comprehensive form of communication used by the deaf that employs all of the grammatical complexities of spoken languages. Rules govern the syntax and grammar of signing, allowing rich verbal communication in the absence of spoken or heard words. There is no universal sign language. Different countries have their own versions. Further, the sign language of a given country is not directly related to the spoken language of that country. For instance, although an English speaker can get along fine in the United States, Australia, Canada, or Great Britain, a person who uses American Sign Language (ASL) cannot communicate with those who use British Sign Language. These are two distinct languages wholly independent of the rules of the English language.

Like spoken language, sign language can be divided into varying levels of complexity. The most basic level of sign language includes hand and arm positions that help to form words, similar to letters and phonemes of spoken language. These gestures include the shape and orientation of the hands, and the location of the hands and arms with respect to the

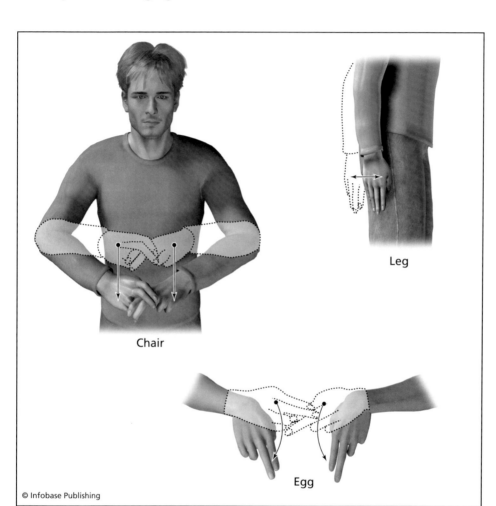

Figure 6.1 ASL signs consist of hand shapes, positioning, and movement. Some signs use the same hand shape but a different movement.

signer's body. At the next level are movements that accompany each gesture, helping to define words. The subtleties of these movements are very important. For example, the ASL signs for the words "train," "chair," "egg," and "tape" all use the same hand shape, orientation to the body, and location in space, but the movement that accompanies each differentiates them (Figure

6.1). This could be compared to the words "tarp" and "part" in English. These words neither sound the same nor mean the same thing simply because they contain the same letters.

Modifications of complete signs can affect the interpretation of words. In English, adding an ending like "ing" or "ed" to a word indicates a specific tense, and adding a prepositional phrase can clarify meaning (for instance, "to them"). In sign language, adding specific motions to signs alters their meaning in similar ways. For instance, the addition of a rolling gesture to most verbs in ASL changes the verb to mean occurring continuously, for instance from "cry" to "crying continuously." Further, though somewhat different from spoken languages, syntactical rules also exist in signing that enable the signer to explain who did what to whom. For example, in the English language, we use word order with specific verb forms to indicate subject and object: "Bill threw the ball to Andrea," or "The ball was thrown to Andrea by Bill." In sign language, these relationships are expressed using spatial information. Each character in a dialogue has his or her own unique spatial location with respect to the signer. By indicating the proper positions in relation to the action being described, the observer can understand whether Bill threw the ball to Andrea or whether Andrea threw the ball to Bill.

Given that fluent signing depends so heavily on precise movements performed in proper spatial orientation, one might imagine that the brain relies heavily on regions that are involved in visual processing, spatial relationships, and hand/arm motor control in order to process sign language. Scientists wondered whether the language centers of deaf individuals that communicate through sign language were distinct from the language centers in the brains of individuals who use spoken language. Some hypothesized that sign language users have language centers located in the right hemisphere. By comparing how the brain processes sign language and spoken languages, scientists have learned more about how the brain handles different aspects of language.

DEFICITS IN SIGN LANGUAGE

Early attempts to assess the brain regions involved in sign language were similar to those used for spoken language. Scientists examined deaf patients who suffered brain damage and assessed any language deficits that developed from damage. Loss of function information was correlated with the damaged areas. After studying the sign language abilities of injured deaf patients, scientists realized that the language deficits that followed brain trauma could be grouped into the same general deficits that occur in patients who use spoken language: language comprehension and language production. One patient, for example, could produce properly formed signs, but the sentences that she created were disjointed and incomprehensible. This is much like a hearing patient who is able to speak words but forms incoherent sentences. Another deaf patient suffering from brain damage, though fully able to understand sign language that she saw, was unable to form proper signs. Only with great effort could she produce approximately correct signs, and typically she was able to express only one-word signs to communicate. Her deficit is much like that of the hearing patient, Tan, described by Broca, who understood words spoken to him but who could not produce speech of his own (see Chapter 4).

When scientists examined the brain regions linked with these sign language deficits, they were surprised to realize that the deaf patients had injuries in Broca's area and Wernicke's area, just like hearing patients with analogous deficits in spoken language. This suggested to researchers that specific areas of the brain contribute to language and that these areas are not necessarily dependent on hearing.

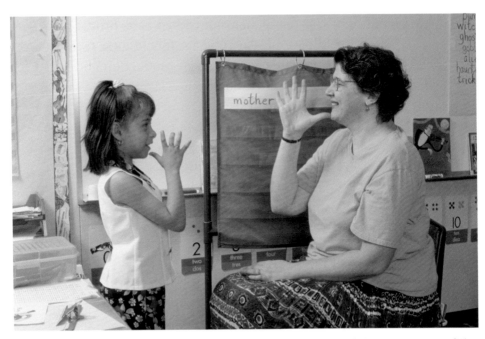

Figure 6.2 Communication in sign language utilizes many of the same areas of the brain that are required for spoken languages.

REGIONS OF THE BRAIN INVOLVED IN SIGN LANGUAGE

The majority of brain regions involved in processing sign language are analogous to those used in processing spoken language (Figure 6.2). As with hearing individuals, most deaf individuals utilize the left hemisphere of the brain for language tasks. Thus, damage to the left hemisphere is often associated with subsequent deficits in sign language. Conversely, damage to the right hemisphere in deaf individuals typically has little effect on language ability, as with hearing patients, despite the fact that sign language has such complex spatial aspects. In the Wada test, in which one half of the brain is silenced with a drug, delivery of the drug to the left hemisphere, but not to the right, abolishes sign language ability, just as it abolishes spoken language ability.

As exemplified by the deaf patients described here, Broca's area and Wernicke's area have similar language functions in the deaf as they do in hearing people: speech/sign production and language comprehension. This left hemisphere lateralization holds true even for individuals who have been deaf from birth and have never been exposed to spoken language, suggesting that these areas of the brain are truly language centers, rather than

Language in Non-Human Primates: Is It Truly Language?

Scientists hope to learn more about human language development by studying whether and how non-human primates learn and use language. Scientists also hope to better understand the similarities between humans and other primates in the ways they think and communicate. Though non-human primates are unable to form spoken language, researchers have successfully trained chimpanzees to use simple sign language.

One language-trained primate is Kanzi. Researchers tried unsuccessfully to teach Kanzi's adoptive mother to use a keyboard containing symbols. Though Kanzi's mother never developed any language during her training, Kanzi, who was watching, picked up a sizeable vocabulary. When Kanzi's trainers realized his ability, they began to teach Kanzi more words. By the age of 6 years, Kanzi knew over 200 signs and constructed simple sentences by combining them. He responded to commands. For example, when his trainers told him to "give the dog a shot," Kanzi injected his stuffed dog with a syringe.

Other primates have been taught to use words. The chimpanzee Washoe also learned over 200 signs through imitation locations that develop as a result of their proximity to auditory or facial motor regions.

Hearing individuals who suffer brain damage that impairs their use of spoken language are sometimes able to learn to communicate through sign language, in spite of the fact that most regions involved in processing sign language are the same as those involved in processing spoken language. This information

and training and was able to make simple word combinations in novel contexts. For example, she learned the word "more" in relation to tickling but then applied "more" to other situations. Washoe adopted an infant chimp named Loulis. As a young chimp, Loulis was not trained in sign language by humans but nevertheless picked up around 50 signs by learning from other chimps.

This use of "language" by chimpanzees, however, is not accepted as true language ability. Chimpanzees do not learn large vocabularies as readily as human children. They only combine a few words at a time and with no particular syntactic structure, compared to human children, who learn to string many words together to express complex ideas and even stories. Many feel that primates use signs mainly to receive rewards and that their language use is no different than pressing a button in order to receive a treat from a trainer. For this reason, primate language is studied primarily by evolutionists seeking to know how the human brain might have developed its complex language capacities suggests that the conceptual aspects of language are stored in regions of the brain separate from the regions that are responsible for executing the audiovisual aspects of language. The differences that have been observed in brain processing of heard versus sign language are primarily due to input and output (taking in auditory versus visual information and producing speech versus signs), rather than in the language content itself. For example, imaging studies used to determine the parts of the brain that are specific for sign language processing show that sign language recruits posterior occipito-temporal regions more heavily than spoken language. These occipito-temporal regions may help to process the movement components of sign language. The language comprehension aspects of language, however, are essentially the same for signed and spoken language. Damage to subcortical regions of the brain involved in speech formation result in disruptions of speech that have nothing to do with other aspects of language processing. For example, a young boy with a form of epilepsy that disrupts language became mute by the age of 6. Nevertheless, he was able to learn to communicate effectively using sign language. His illness affected execution regions of speech but did not involve higher cortical areas required for comprehension.

SECOND LANGUAGES

In addition to the study of sign language, studying how the brain processes a second language may also provide information about the function of human language centers. Unlike the acquisition of a first language, which occurs automatically without the need for formal training, second languages are learned through conscious effort, much like reading and writing are learned after the words and meaning of a first language have been acquired. Studying second language acquisition may reveal

Figure 6.3 Children learn a second language more easily than adults. In this photograph, a boy uses a multimedia computer program to learn French.

brain regions that are involved in conscious learning versus those that are active during less formal acquisition.

Although there is no critical period for second language acquisition as there is for first language acquisition, there does seem to be an optimal period. If a child learns a second language prior to 7 to 12 years of age, the language will be learned more easily and spoken more fluently, with less of an accent (Figure 6.3). That is not to say, however, that it is impossible to learn a second language later in life. It just takes more effort. Also, unlike first language acquisition, second language acquisition does not necessarily follow predictable patterns. Second language learners will not go through periods of predictable errors in the way that children do when acquiring a first language. Instead, there is wide variation in the progress of second language acquisition, and the errors frequently made are unique to individuals. Scientists wonder whether this means that different regions of the brain are involved in establishing a second language than those active during first language acquisition. Though this question remains unanswered, research has given us some clues.

One phenomenon of language that makes second language acquisition so challenging is the way the brain organizes the phonemes of a person's native language. In Chapter 3, we noted that babies start out making a variety of sounds when they babble, but as they begin to acquire their native language, they select only those sounds that are used in their own language. If a sound isn't used in a person's native language, that person may not even be able to hear its distinction from another sound in a different language. An example is the consonant sounds "l" and "r" used in the English language. The Japanese language uses "r" sounds but not the "l" sound. Japanese infants are able to discriminate between the English "r" and "l," but as they learn their native language, they lose this ability to detect the differences in these sounds. When native Japanese speakers learn the English language, they find "l" indistinguishable from "r," so the words "read" and "lead" would sound the same to them. Even though they learn that these sounds are distinct in English, it is difficult for them to pronounce words containing "l" correctly. This suggests that the brain has a large amount of plasticity in its language centers at early ages but that plasticity is reduced later on. Language acquisition itself may disrupt some of this plasticity, influencing the sounds we are able to perceive and form. Presumably, neural connections that represent the phonemes of a person's native language are reinforced, while connections that are not used in the native language are lost. Some scientists think that the development of a particular language shapes the brain in a way that actually influences our ability to think and to interpret the world.

Two factors seem to impact the way the brain processes second languages: the age when the second language was learned and the proficiency level of the second language. One brain imaging study compared regions of the frontal lobe that are used in processing first and second languages. The authors examined brain activity in two groups of people that were both proficient in their second language. One group of subjects learned their second language at a very young age; the other group learned later in life. The group that had learned a second language at a young age used the same regions of the frontal lobe to process both languages. The group that learned their second language later in life used distinct regions of the frontal lobe to process each language.

The influence of age on second language acquisition is presumably due to a greater ability of the brain to restructure itself at a young age than at a more mature age. Kuniyoshi Sakai, a scientist who uses brain imaging to study language, has suggested that two distinct aspects of language are subject to separate sensitive periods: word meaning and sentence meaning. Brain imaging studies suggest that these functions of language are processed by distinct but interconnected regions of the brain and that these areas are utilized differently by humans for processing first or second languages, depending on the age of acquisition and proficiency level of the second language. The most marked difference in processing between a first and a second language occurs in subregions of a part of the cerebral cortex called the inferior frontal gyrus (IFG): the triangular and orbital regions. The IFG has been linked to grammatical processing in people using both spoken languages and sign language. When people are learning a second language, this area is especially active, more so than during use of the native language. After years of study, when the subjects are more proficient in their second language, the activity in this region is comparable whether the subjects are using their native or their second language.

LESSONS OF SIGN AND SECOND LANGUAGES

The study of sign language and second languages has contributed to our understanding of the way the brain processes language. These studies emphasize that cortical areas contributing to language are predetermined language centers, participating in language independent of its mode, whether spoken or signed. Cortical areas involved in comprehension are interconnected with, but distinct from, subcortical regions necessary for speech. Portions of the language centers contribute more prominently to learning language than they do in using language after it has been acquired proficiently.

■ **Learn more about languages and second languages** Search the Internet for *American Sign Language, second language acquisition,* and *chimp sign language.*

7 | Language and Thought

An ongoing debate in the research of language involves the role of language in organized thought. Some argue that language itself is necessary for complex thought and planning, and that the advances of modern civilization occurred only after the development of language provided humans with new opportunities. Others believe that language is not necessary for thought but rather is simply an organized mode for sharing thought with others. A part of this debate is based on the Sapir-Whorf hypothesis, which proposes that thought is dependent on language. Much research has attempted to prove or disprove the Sapir-Whorf hypothesis, with the hope of understanding how the brain is able to achieve and express thought.

SAPIR-WHORF HYPOTHESIS

Influential publications of the anthropologist Edward Sapir and his student Benjamin Whorf detail what is now called the Sapir-Whorf hypothesis, which posits that the language a person uses influences his or her interpretation of the world and his or her behavior. The idea was not a new one. A sixth-century Indian philosopher named Bhartrihari argued that language and thought are essentially one and the same. For centuries, people have discussed the ways in which language and thought seem to be inextricably linked. Sapir and Whorf were influenced by the German anthropologist Franz Boas, who traveled to the United States and studied the languages used by Native Americans. Boas noted that the culture and lifestyles of populations were reflected in their language. Sapir contemplated this, noting that languages are complex systems and that the rules governing them seem interwoven with the culture and thought of those who use them.

> Human beings do not live in the objective world alone, nor alone in the world of social activity as ordinarily understood, but are very much at the mercy of the particular language which has become the medium of expression for their society. . . . The fact of the matter is that the "real world" is to a large extent built up on the language habits of the group. No two languages are ever sufficiently similar to be considered as representing the same social reality. The worlds in which different societies live are distinct worlds, not merely the same world with different labels attached. . . . We see and hear and otherwise experience very largely as we do because the language habits of our community predispose certain choices of interpretation.[4]

Sapir suspected that language might influence or even determine an individual's thoughts. Whorf expanded Sapir's ideas by examining specific grammatical rules of languages and how they influenced thought. Whorf was particularly interested in the Native American Hopi language. He was surprised that this language does not use words for time. Rather than describing things in terms of yesterday, today, now, tomorrow, or the future, the Hopi tend to think of things in terms of processes. Whorf concluded that the Hopi perception of the world must be very different than that of people whose native language place emphasis on time. The following excerpt explains Whorf's conclusions about the influence of language on thought:

> We dissect nature along lines laid down by our native languages. . . . The world is presented in a kaleido-scopic flux of impressions which has to be organized by our minds—and this means largely by the linguistic systems in our minds. We cut nature up, organize it into concepts, and ascribe significances as we do, largely because we are parties to an agreement to organize it in this way—an agreement that holds throughout our speech community and is codified in the patterns of our language.[5]

Most people who study language believe neither that language fully determines thought nor that thought is completely free of the influences of language. One simple example that argues against language determining thought is that people sometimes have trouble finding words to explain a concept they understand. If thought were dependent on language, then they would never have a thought that could not be adequately expressed in words. Alternately, an argument that suggests that language influences thought is based on people's stated perception of color. All languages have a set of words to denote basic colors. English uses red, orange, yellow, green, blue, and purple, as well as brown, gray, black, and white. Colors such as peach, mint, or lavender are not considered basic. Not all languages, however, denote the same basic colors. For instance, some tribal languages have only two basic colors, while other languages have as many as 11. Some languages do not have a word for the color orange (for example, the language of the Iñupiat, native people of Alaska; the Native American Zuni dialect; or the Cebuano dialect of the Philippines). If you asked a person who speaks one of these languages to categorize a group of items by color, he would lump an orange and a banana in the same group, while an English speaker would separate them into two groups. This is an example of how the conventions of language can influence the thought and behavior of individuals.

EMPIRICAL ASSESSMENT

There are two main problems in analyzing evidence that language influences thought. First, it is nearly impossible to determine if the examples people have used to argue the point really indicate the thoughts of an individual. For instance, one can consider the example of words for basic colors explained previously. Individuals will classify objects by color in different ways depending on the words they have available to describe color. This indeed seems to show an influence of language in people's thoughts and actions, but this does not necessarily mean that the person who has fewer words with which to categorize colors actually perceives color differently than an individual with more words at his or her disposal. If you asked either individual to arrange the objects along the color spectrum, you may find that each of them arranges the objects in the same way, moving from what English speakers call red, through the spectrum to violet. It is unclear whether the color categorization task really determines an individual's thoughts about color. Second, it is difficult to know whether the thoughts and culture of a population influenced the words within its language in the first place; language could influence thought or, conversely, thought could influence language.

In addition to differences in words for time and color, languages also vary in their words for shapes and number. Two recent studies have explored the thought/language relationship by looking at how infants respond to spatial relationships and how people without many words for numbers respond to numerical representations.

Thought in Infants

In a set of experiments with five-month-old, preverbal infants, the psychologists Susan Hespos and Elizabeth Spelke assessed infants' abilities to detect categories of spatial relationships not conventionally used in the native language of their parents. They were interested in linguistic differences between Korean and English. In English, speakers tend to describe spatial relationships between objects using the words "in" and "on" while in Korean, speakers tend to describe objects in contact with each other as having a tight fit or a loose fit. For example, in Korean, a cap on a pen is defined as a tight fit, while a pen on a table is defined as a loose fit. English speakers instead tend to think of coffee in a mug or a mug on a table.

The researchers showed babies of English-speaking parents a series of objects all having a tight fit or a loose fit relationship. They monitored the amount of time babies spent looking at these objects when they were presented. Then they switched and showed the babies a set of objects with the opposite relationship (a loose fit if they had been looking at a tight fit previously or vice versa). They observed how long the babies looked at the objects with the new spatial relationship. Looking longer would suggest that the babies were interested in something novel about the objects, while looking for a comparable time would indicate that the babies perceived the new objects as more of what they had already seen. Hespos and Spelke found that babies looked longer at the objects in the new category of tight or loose fit relationship than they did after seeing a series of objects all in one class. In contrast, English-speaking adults were less likely to pick up on the change in the spatial relationship of the presented objects, though Korean-speaking adults readily noticed the relationship.

These findings suggest two things about language. First, language is not necessary for thought. Babies notice categorical relationships in their environment before they develop language.

Language, therefore, may develop out of categorical distinctions that the brain uses in order to interpret the world, rather than vice versa. Second, language influences the details that adults perceive. English-speaking adults not accustomed to thinking of tight or loose fit relationships between objects are less likely to notice the categorization. It is not that they can't recognize this relationship. Some English speakers notice it on their own, and others easily perceive the relationship once it has been pointed out to them. English-speaking people, however, simply perceive this relationship less readily than Korean-speaking people, who describe objects in this manner regularly. Thus, language does not determine thought but may influence it.

Numerical Assessment Without Words for Numbers

Another interesting set of experiments regarding the interplay of language and thought was performed by Peter Gordon. Gordon was interested in how people without an extensive vocabulary for numbers would perceive quantity. The Pirahã culture of Brazil has a limited set of words to describe quantity: approximately one, approximately two, and many. He asked the Pirahã people to participate in numerical tasks of varying degrees of difficulty. In one task, he arranged a set of AA batteries in a pattern and asked the subjects to copy the pattern with their own set of batteries. In another task, he asked the subjects to draw a line representing each battery in an array. This was a more difficult task for the Pirahã, as they do not use drawing or writing in their culture. The subjects did a good job on the numerical tasks when they involved quantities up to 3. Beyond quantities of 4, however, their performance began to deteriorate. As the numbers the subjects were asked to assess got higher, their responses also got higher, though they were not accurate assessments. This suggests that the subjects were making a rough approximation of the "many" items they were observing.

Nevertheless, the subjects struggled to discern between numbers higher than 3. Even when incentives of rewards were offered for accurate discrimination between 3 items or 4 items, the subjects' correct responses were around the level of chance. This study provides evidence that in the absence of words to describe a concept, people may have difficulty perceiving the concept itself. Accordingly, the evidence supports the idea that language may influence thought more strongly than typically expected. The Pirahã study is unable to determine, however, whether the lack of numerical vocabulary in the Pirahã language has influenced their culture or vice versa.

BEYOND SAPIR-WHORF

The Sapir-Whorf hypothesis predicts that language influences thought and emphasizes differences in behaviors of people with different verbal representations of the world, but the hypothesis does not address the issue of thought in people who have never developed language at all. This is a different but related issue regarding how language affects thought. Clearly, thought is possible without language, since studies such as the one by Hespos and Spelke indicate that preverbal infants are actively assessing the world around them. Thought also is evident in animals that show problem-solving abilities in order to obtain a food reward. For instance, a dog that sees food behind a glass, after realizing he cannot get at the food by going through the glass, will eventually go around the glass. The dog maintains a memory of the food for long enough to get around the obstruction, even though the dog has no verbal ability to construct a plan. The dog does not say to himself, "I will stop looking at the food and find a way around this glass. Hopefully, I will be able to find a way around, and the food will still be there for me to eat it." Nevertheless, the dog eventually manages to get the food reward.

Is thought without words, though, equivalent to verbal thought? Joseph, the deaf child described in Chapter 2, never fully developed language. His ability to form plans and to consider abstractions appeared limited. Possibly, acquisition of language enables the brain to coordinate complicated levels of analysis. If this were true, it might account for the incredible advances that occurred in human civilization concurrent with the development of language. On the other hand, there are numerous examples of individuals who have lost their language ability following brain damage but who, nevertheless, perform well on nonverbal portions of IQ tests. Also, children with language development impairments similarly may show normal intelligence.

The relationship between language and human thought is still the subject of debate and speculation. Future studies may begin to examine the regions of the brain that are active in tasks such as those used in the Pirahā study. These studies may reveal whether people without vocabulary for a concept use the same brain regions to approach tasks as people with extensive vocabulary related to the task. For now, the role that language plays in the intricacies of the human mind remains, in large part, a mystery.

■ **Learn more about language and thought** Search the Internet for *Sapir-Whorf hypothesis* and *Franz Boas.*

8 | Speech Disorders

There are many speech and language impairments, some due to genetic or developmental problems and others due to brain damage. Over the course of this and the following two chapters, we will discuss some of these disorders. We begin in this chapter with impairments specific to speech —stuttering and spasmodic dysphonia. In Chapter 9, we will discuss speech impairments that result from brain damage, and in Chapter 10, we will consider disorders that are not primarily disorders of speech and language but that have a language component.

STUTTERING

Stuttering (also called stammering) is a speech disorder in which fluency is disrupted by repetitions and prolongations in syllables, sounds, and words. An individual who stutters often has difficulty starting words. Normal speech production is a complicated process that requires the brain to coordinate a number of muscles in a precise manner, including those involved in respiration, vocalization, and articulation (involving the throat, palate, tongue, lips, and teeth). The brain regulates these muscles by processing sensory feedback that comes from hearing and touch. Though the causes of stuttering are not yet known, it is believed that stuttering occurs when there are disruptions in the way that the brain coordinates the various components necessary for the production of speech.

There are three classes of stuttering: developmental, neurogenic, and psychogenic. Developmental stuttering begins in childhood and may persist into adulthood. It has been hypothesized that this form of stuttering occurs when the child's speech/language ability lags behind the child's verbal needs. These children appear to be stuck as they struggle to find and form the proper words to express their thoughts. Neurogenic, by definition, refers to conditions pertaining to the brain and nerves. Neurogenic stuttering occurs because of signaling problems between the brain and nerves and the muscles required to execute speech, leaving the brain unable to coordinate the components required for fluid speech. Persistent developmental stuttering is a neurogenic form of stuttering. Neurogenic stuttering may also develop later in life, following stroke or other brain injuries, or as a result of drug abuse. Stuttering that develops later in life contrasts with persistent developmental stuttering. Typically, neurogenic stuttering occurs throughout speech patterns, while developmental stuttering typically occurs at just the beginning of speech. Further, individuals who develop a stutter following injury or drug abuse typically are unconcerned about their speech disability, while those with developmental stuttering find the disability to be a source of worry and embarrassment. Psychogenic conditions have no known underlying abnormalities in the brain and are believed to originate in the mind during thought or emotional processing. Psychogenic stuttering is believed to be very rare. This form of stuttering occasionally develops in people with mental illness or following extreme cases of mental stress. The stuttering has no apparent neurological basis; speech circuitry was intact in these individuals prior to the onset of their stuttering, and no known injuries occurred that would disrupt that intact circuitry. Another possible form of stuttering has been reported in individuals who communicate with sign language, exhibited by preservations and lack of coordination in movements as well as repeated syllables, but little research is available on this subject.

Incidence of Stuttering

Stuttering is believed to affect between 1 and 2% of the overall population[6], though the incidence is much higher in children between the ages of 2 and 6 who are developing language. In children, the incidence of stuttering has been estimated to be as high as 15%. Many of these children (estimated at two-thirds or more) outgrow the disability. Females, especially, are likely to outgrow developmental stuttering, while males are three times more likely to stutter than females and are less likely to outgrow their stuttering. Many well-known orators, actors, and singers have outgrown childhood stuttering, including Winston Churchill, James Earl Jones, Marilyn Monroe, Jimmy Stewart, Bruce Willis, Carly Simon, and Mel Tillis.

Causes of Stuttering

Stuttering seems to have a genetic basis, though as of yet no "stuttering gene" has been determined. Stuttering runs in families. In some families, there are multiple cases of persistent stuttering. In these families, males and females have more equivalent likelihood of developing stuttering problems. In families with sporadic stuttering, however, males are much more likely to develop stuttering. Among monozygotic (or identical) twins, if one twin stutters, there is a 90% chance that the sibling will also stutter. This percentage falls to 20% for dizygotic (or fraternal) twins. Family history is also predictive of people who will recover from their stuttering and people who will have persistent stuttering. The form of stuttering that individuals recover from, then, is not likely a milder form of persistent stuttering but a distinct form of the disability.

Researchers have found that slower speech improves fluency in those who stutter. Stuttering likewise improves when those who stutter read aloud along with other individuals (an activity called choral speech). Choral speech tends to be slower than the speech of individuals. Scientists hypothesize that the threshold for the maximum rate of speech (the rate above which errors occur) in stuttering individuals is lower than that for non-stuttering individuals. People who stutter tend to become distressed as they perceive their errors, causing them to tense their muscles. Consciously relaxing the muscles of their body also helps to improve speech fluency. Slowed speech and relaxation strategies are commonly used as fluency-enhancing therapies for children who stutter.

Some of the first evidence of the systems involved in stuttering was provided by experiments assessing auditory feedback. In 1975, researchers at the University of Liverpool in England found that speech fluency is inversely correlated with auditory feedback: minimizing the auditory feedback arriving in the brains of those who stutter improves their speech fluency. Minimizing auditory feedback is accomplished by delivering sound through headphones while stuttering subjects are speaking, diminishing their ability to hear their own voices as they speak. Disruption in feedback is more effective when delivered to the right ear than the left ear, suggesting that a lateralized process may contribute to the dysfunction, producing stuttering. Another study used a delayed feedback device. This device delays the auditory feedback of a person's own voice by several milliseconds, so that the speaker does not hear his/her own voice until after a syllable has been pronounced. This strategy markedly improves the speech fluency of those who stutter. Interestingly, delayed auditory feedback disrupts the speech of individuals who do not stutter.

Brain imaging studies have provided some of the first information about the regions of the brain involved in stuttering. Some general differences in regional function during language tasks have been observed between those who stutter and non-stuttering controls. First, there is less left hemispheric dominance for language in those who stutter than in those who do not. Increased activity has been observed in the motor regions involved in speech, while decreased activity has been observed in language regions in those who stutter. When individuals who stutter engage in choral speaking, which minimizes stuttering, activity in the left hemisphere is enhanced to levels observed in non-stuttering individuals, and motor areas are quieted. Researchers believe that choral speech somehow bypasses some of the circuitry that occurs in the brain's subcortical speech regions and shifts processing to the cortical speech regions (including the frontal and temporal lobes and Broca's area), which are fully intact in these individuals. The enhanced activity observed in the right hemisphere during the speech of stuttering subjects is hypothesized to be compensatory activity, meaning that it is a result of stuttering, rather than a cause. The brain may attempt to enhance speech processing by recruiting these areas in the absence of normal left hemisphere activity.

Treatment of Stuttering

Overproduction of the neurotransmitter **dopamine** may underlie the circuitry signaling problem, because drugs that block dopaminergic receptors in the brain have improved stuttering (Figure 8.1). Despite their efficacy, these drugs (such as haloperidol, also called Haldol) are not a favored method for treating stuttering because they have side effects that prevent their long-term use. One troubling side effect of haloperidol is a condition called **tardive dyskinesia**. This involves involuntary and uncontrolled movements of the mouth, tongue, cheeks, jaw, or arms

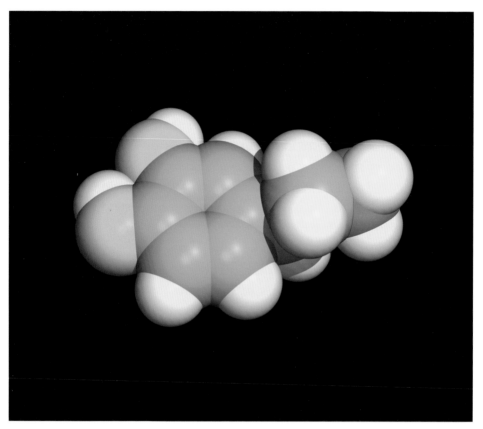

Figure 8.1 The neurotransmitter dopamine consists of carbon *(green)*, oxygen *(blue)*, nitrogen *(magenta)*, and hydrogen *(yellow)* atoms. Overproduction of dopamine may lead to stuttering and psychotic illnesses such as schizophrenia.

and legs. The condition does not improve after a patient stops taking the drug. In the case of stuttering, the possible side effects of the treatment may outweigh the benefit. Newer versions of drugs that minimize dopamine signaling (such as risperidone and olanzapine) may eventually prove more beneficial.

In the absence of medications, the main strategy for the treatment of stuttering includes therapy. The efficacy of therapy is limited, given that persistent stuttering appears to be due to altered function in the speech centers of the brain. For individuals with persistent stuttering, it isn't possible to learn not to stutter, but the fluency of speech can be improved. Rather than eliminating all stuttering, therapies for individuals with persistent stuttering include implementation of speech strategies that minimize stuttering, relaxation techniques that aid stuttering individuals to release themselves from a stuttering pattern, and emotional support. Those who stutter often withdraw from social situations in which they may need to speak, and they are often hesitant to speak to strangers. Therapy for stuttering often includes efforts to help those who stutter to accept their disability and to participate fully in activities in spite of this. Alternately, electronic devices that alter auditory feedback, similar to those used in the experiments described previously, are available. Those who have used the devices, however, tend to view them as too cumbersome to provide a realistic therapeutic option. Future research may provide more promising treatments.

SPASMODIC DYSPHONIA

Spasmodic dysphonia is a speech disorder affecting one or more muscles of the larynx (Figure 8.2). Involuntary movements of the larynx disrupt speech by causing the voice to break or by giving the voice a strained, strangled, or groaning quality. The severity of the disorder varies. In mild instances, an individual may have occasional difficulty saying some words. In more severe cases, the disability may interfere with an individual's ability to communicate. Spasmodic dysphonia may go away for hours or even days and then return again. Being stressed or tired can exacerbate the problem. There are three types of spasmodic dysphonia, defined by the specific affected muscles of the larynx: adductor, abductor, or mixed.

In adductor spasmodic dysphonia, muscle spasms cause the vocal cords to stiffen and close together. This reduces the ability

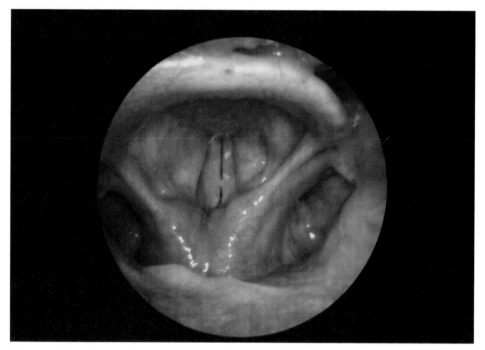

Figure 8.2 The vocal cords are closed in this photograph of a healthy larynx. Changes in tension of the vocal cords result in sounds of different pitch.

of the vocal folds to form vibrations and sound. The speaker's words are interrupted or difficult to initiate. The voice sounds strained, and it appears that the individual is speaking with great effort. When the speaker is whispering, speaking at a high pitch, or speaking while breathing in, singing, or laughing, the spasms rarely occur.

Abductor spasmodic dysphonia is due to muscle spasms that cause the vocal folds to open suddenly, which also reduces the ability of the vocal folds to vibrate and produce sound. Air escapes the vocal cords through the open position and gives a breathy, weak sound to the voice. Modifying the voice, as with adductor spasmodic dysphonia (singing, and so on), reduces the instance of muscle spasms and improves the condition.

Mixed spasmodic dysphonia involves both the muscles that open and the muscles that close the vocal folds. The vocal quality of individuals with mixed spasmodic dysphonia will have aspects of both adductor and abductor spasmodic dysphonia, and their condition will be similarly ameliorated by the same vocal changes that minimize the other forms of spasmodic dysphonia.

Spasmodic dysphonia often occurs along with other movement disorders. These disorders, including tardive dyskinesia, typically involve involuntary movements of the face, jaw, lips, and tongue as well as the neck or body. One movement disorder that often accompanies spasmodic dysphonia is blephorospasm, defined by excessive blinking and involuntary, forceful eye closure.

Incidence of Spasmodic Dysphonia

There is little information regarding the prevalence of spasmodic dysphonia. The condition can affect people of all ages, though it is typically seen in people between the ages of 30 and 50. Approximately twice as many females as males exhibit symptoms. Spasmodic dysphonia sometimes runs in families. A small percentage of individuals with spasmodic dysphonia report family members with similar conditions, so the condition is believed to have a genetic component. Future information regarding the incidence of spasmodic dysphonia will help to clarify the potential genetic components of the disorder.

Causes of Spasmodic Dysphonia

As with stuttering, the underlying causes of spasmodic dysphonia are unknown. Because many individuals diagnosed with the condition are often able to speak in a normal way, spasmodic dysphonia was initially believed to be a psychogenic condition. Modern research, however, suggests that spasmodic dysphonia is actually a neurogenic condition, having its roots in the neural systems that are responsible for coordinating vocalization.

Brain imaging studies of individuals with spasmodic dysphonia show abnormalities in processing in either the cortical language centers or the basal ganglia and cranial nerves. Some studies have detected lesions in cortical regions in about half of the subjects with spasmodic dysphonia, including the left frontal/temporal regions, areas of the medial frontal cortex, and posterior regions of the right temporal/parietal regions. Another 25% of patients show abnormalities in both the cortical and the subcortical regions involved in vocalization. Less than 10% have abnormalities in subcortical regions alone. Researchers have hypothesized that head injuries, multi-infarct microvascular disease (blockage or ruptures of blood vessels in or leading to the brain), or exposure to neurotoxins might lead to the development of subcortical lesions. Interestingly, in about 16% of patients with spasmodic dysphonia, no disruptions in either cortical or subcortical processing can be identified, so the cause of their disability remains unclear.[7]

Treatment of Spasmodic Dysphonia

Although there is no cure for spasmodic dysphonia, there are treatments that alleviate the symptoms. Historically, most patients received psychological therapy that helped them to accept their disorder along with job counseling that helped patients find employment compatible with their speaking difficulties. Mild cases were, and still are, often managed with voice therapy alone. Relaxation techniques, breath control, and modifications of pitch or loudness all improve vocalizations.

More severe cases have been treated surgically or, more recently, with injections of a toxin. The surgical procedure used to treat spasmodic dysphonia involves severing the cranial nerve that stimulates the vocal folds, called the recurrent laryngeal nerve. This procedure improves the voice quality of many patients. The treatment is problematic, however, because in about two-thirds of the patients who receive this surgery, the improvement is not permanent. The improvement may last from 6 months to several years before the condition begins to worsen again. In some individuals, the condition becomes even worse after this period of improvement following surgery.

In an alternate treatment, small amounts of **botulinum toxin,** the toxic compound produced by the bacterium *Clostridium botulinum*, are injected directly into the facial muscles of the larynx. This toxin binds to nerve terminals where they connect with muscles. It blocks the ability of the nerves to stimulate muscle contractions. When injected into the muscles of the vocal folds of patients with spasmodic dysphonia, the toxin improves the vocal quality. As with the surgical technique, this treatment is also temporary. Botulinum toxin injections reduce symptoms for 3 to 4 months, after which the condition begins to deteriorate gradually. The toxin may be reinjected success-fully, however, so this treatment is the most promising to date for those who suffer from spasmodic dysphonia.

■ Learn more about speech disorders Search the Internet for *stuttering, spasmodic dysphonia,* and *tardive dyskinesia.*

Speech and Language Impairments Resulting from Brain Damage

9

A number of speech impairments develop as a result of brain damage from either injury or disease. Stroke, brain tumor, or other traumatic brain injuries (such as gunshot wounds or blows to the head) may disrupt portions of the speech centers, leaving individuals with problems producing speech or comprehending language. In severe forms, these speech disorders may have a devastating impact on an individual's ability to participate in society.

APHASIA

Aphasia is a partial or total loss of the ability to articulate or comprehend language. Those who suffer from aphasia may have difficulty with expressive language (speaking), receptive language (comprehension), or both. Heard and spoken language is impaired as well as reading and writing. The severity of aphasia depends on the location and extent of brain damage. Aphasia may improve over time, but it is sometimes permanent. People with a severe form of aphasia may understand almost nothing of what is spoken to them, and their communications may be limited to words such as "yes" or "no" or common social words such as "hi" and "thanks." Those with milder forms of aphasia may be able to carry on normal conversations in most contexts, having difficulty only when language is complex.

Broca's Aphasia

Broca's aphasia is acquired following damage to the frontal lobe of the brain, the site of Broca's area. Individuals with this type of aphasia typically speak in short phrases, leaving out function words or other short words such as "is," "and," "of," or "the." Typically these individuals understand the speech of others and realize the limitations of their own speech, which may be a source of frustration. Sometimes this type of aphasia is accompanied by paralysis of an arm and/or leg because the damaged area also affects the motor regions situated nearby.

Wernicke's Aphasia

A second form of aphasia results from damage to the temporal lobe, where Wernicke's area is located. These individuals may speak in long, full sentences, but their words may be unintelligible. These aphasics may include nonsense words in their sentences as well. Individuals with damage to Wernicke's area typically have difficulty in language comprehension, so they may be unaware of the flaws in their language.

Global Aphasia

Global aphasia occurs when individuals have extensive damage to the language centers of the brain. Often, the ability to comprehend and form language is severely limited in these individuals. In addition to the symptoms already described, some people with aphasia may have trouble thinking of words. For instance, they won't be able to think of the name for an object, even though they can explain its use. This phenomenon is referred to as **anomia**. Others may make errors in word order. Still others may switch words, often words of loosely related meaning. For instance, they may confuse the word "bed" with the word "table." People with aphasia may also switch sounds within words, for example, calling a "dishwasher" a "wish dasher." If people with aphasia are able to understand language, they may simply need more time than others to process language they read or hear. Comprehending fast-paced language (such as a radio commercial) is difficult, and often figurative language, such as "She really put her foot in her mouth that time" or "He slipped and let the cat out of the bag" will be taken literally.

Incidence of Aphasia

Aphasia is estimated to affect approximately one million people in the United States, with an estimated 80,000 individuals acquiring aphasia each year. Most of these individuals are middle-aged or older, perhaps because damage due to stroke (typically striking later in life) contributes to the numbers of individuals affected with aphasia (Figure 9.1). Aphasia is equally likely to occur in men and women.[8]

Treatment of Aphasia

Some individuals will recover spontaneously from aphasia, while others will not. Recovery depends largely on the extent of brain damage causing the deficit. Minor trauma, such as transient ischemic attacks where blood flow to a region of the brain is disrupted for only a brief period of time, may lead to aphasia that resolves in just hours or days. More extensive damage causes long-term or permanent deficits. Typically, recovery from more serious damage requires a period of about two years. Chances of recovery from aphasia are influenced by the area and extent of brain damage, the age at which the damage occurred, and the overall health of the individual. People with high education levels tend to have a better prognosis than less educated individuals. In situations of ischemic stroke, new drugs delivered shortly after the injury may help to prevent or mitigate subsequent deficits. For example, thrombolytic agents

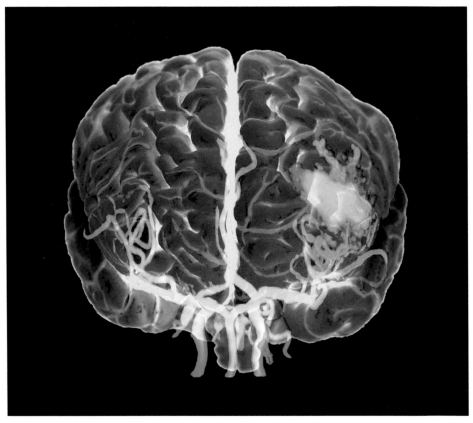

Figure 9.1 This MRI scan shows internal bleeding in a stroke victim's brain. Bleeding in the brain can cause speech disorders such as aphasia.

such as Alteplase help to dissolve blood clots and reestablish blood flow.

Therapy may help to improve symptoms of aphasia. The particular therapeutic strategies used depend on the precise symptoms of the individuals. Group therapies are often used to help people with common disabilities to practice their speech in a group of understanding peers. Therapy often involves family participation to help individuals' loved ones communicate with them.

Ischemic Stroke

The brain relies on blood flow from the heart to provide its cells with adequate oxygen and nutrients needed for survival. Blood flow also clears away carbon dioxide and other waste produced by cells. An ischemic stroke blocks critical blood flow in the brain. Ischemic stroke often occurs as a result of a condition called atherosclerosis, in which deposition of cholesterol narrows the arteries over time. This narrowing of the arteries may cause red blood cells to jam into a clot. If a clot forms in a vessel of the brain and results in a blockage of blood flow, this condition is referred to as thrombotic stroke. Thrombotic stroke constitutes approximately 50% of all ischemic strokes.

The severity of the stroke depends on where the blockage occurs. Blockages that occur in larger vessels responsible for delivering oxygen to wide portions of the brain are particularly harmful. Alternatively, a clot formed in either the heart or one of the body's arteries may dislodge from the region in which it was formed and become lodged in another region, reducing blood flow to the brain. The resulting condition is referred to as embolic stroke. If blood flow in the brain is reduced for more than a few minutes, permanent damage may occur.

Ischemic stroke is one of the leading illnesses that disrupts human language capacity. If a stroke damages one or more of the many regions of the brain involved with language processing, a number of potentially permanent speech and language deficits may result. Recently, new therapeutic strategies for ischemic stroke have been developed, but these are effective only when the stroke is identified and treated quickly following its onset.

DYSARTHRIA

Dysarthria is defined as a difficulty in articulating speech due to weakening or dysfunction of the muscles of the mouth, face, and/or respiratory system, specifically due to brain injury. Symptoms of dysarthria may include slurred speech; speaking softly or barely in a whisper; slowed speech or rapid, mumbled speech; restricted movement of the tongue, lips, and jaw; abnormal rhythm of speech; or altered vocal quality (the speaker may sound stuffy, nasal, hoarse, or breathless). Dysarthria may also include chewing or swallowing difficulty or drooling and poor control of saliva. Dysarthria often accompanies other disorders, such as cerebral palsy, Parkinson's disease, amyotrophic lateral sclerosis (also called Lou Gehrig's disease), Huntington's disease, and multiple sclerosis.

Treatment of Dysarthria

Treatment depends on its cause and the precise symptoms that develop. Therapy is used to help patients articulate more clearly and loudly through exercises in breath support and muscle strengthening or alterations to the speed of speech. Therapy may focus on increasing movement of the mouth, tongue, and lips. Dysarthria does not impair an individual's ability to comprehend language or to form coherent expressions. The problem is strictly due to an inability to control the muscles needed to form speech. Therefore, if these strategies do not sufficiently improve communication, people may use sign language, communicate by writing their ideas, or use electronic or computer-based devices to aid them in expressing themselves. These devices write and produce language.

APRAXIA

Apraxia is another motor disorder affecting speech. Unlike individuals with dysarthria, there is no weakness or paralysis of the muscles involved with speech. Individuals with apraxia instead have difficulty coordinating their speech. They know the words they want to say, but the sounds that they produce don't come out as they intend. Long words are often particularly difficult for these individuals. The errors they make are often inconsistent; sometimes they form particular sounds successfully but other times fail. This may happen over various time frames. For instance, an individual might successfully pronounce a difficult word but subsequently would be unable to repeat the word properly. Alternatively, an individual with apraxia may be able to consistently produce a particular sound or word one day but then may have difficulty with that same sound or word the next day. These individuals hear the errors in their speech as they occur and attempt to fix them, but with limited success.

Apraxia often develops following brain injury, but there is a second, developmental form of apraxia. Though developmental apraxia of speech is believed to be neurogenic in nature, unlike the disorders discussed in Chapter 8, brain imaging studies have been unable to detect any related abnormalities in brain function. Developmental apraxia of speech tends to run in families with a history of language and communication disorders, so this form of apraxia likely has a genetic basis.

Those with apraxia may have a variety of symptoms. They have difficulty imitating the speech sounds of others as well as non-speech movements of the tongue and mouth (for example, they may not be able to stick out their tongue if asked). Often they will have a slow rate of speech and falter as they grasp for the sounds they wish to speak. They may attempt to say a word many times before they successfully pronounce it. The prosody (the melodic rhythms and inflections of their speech) may sound abnormal. Common, automatic expressions such as greetings may be easier for individuals with apraxia to produce.

Figure 9.2 Speech therapists often work with people with apraxia to help them improve their verbal skills.

Treatment of Apraxia

Apraxia often is improved by retraining an individual to create the muscle movements necessary to produce sounds or to link sounds into words (Figure 9.2). Retraining involves extensive repetition of sounds while concentrating on the proper movements necessary to form the sound. Patients also focus on pacing their speech to allow for the extra concentration they may need to properly form and connect sounds. As with dysarthria, individuals with apraxia fully understand language and are able to conceptualize thoughts they would like to express. It is simply a coordination of speech that is disrupted. If therapy cannot sufficiently improve communication, as with dysarthria, the use of sign language, written language on paper, or electronic equipment may enable alternative communication to speech. Apraxia due to brain damage may spontaneously recover with no intervention, though the developmental form of apraxia, in contrast, does not remit on its own.

FOREIGN ACCENT SYNDROME

Following brain damage, patients may develop changes in the phonetic features of their speech, causing them to sound as if they speak with a foreign accent, though the speaker is using his or her native language. English speakers with **foreign accent syndrome** have been described as having French, German, Swedish, Asian, or other accents. Usually listeners mistake individuals with foreign accent syndrome as non-native speakers of their mother language, though they usually have difficulty determining a possible origin of the accent. The stress, rhythm, and intonation of speech may all be modified. Articulations of both consonant and vowel sounds are perturbed, and syllable structure of words may also be modified.

Causes of Foreign Accent Syndrome

Foreign accent syndrome is very rare. Only a few cases have been reported in medical literature. The majority of these patients developed foreign accent syndrome following a stroke, and only a handful of individuals have been described as developing the syndrome following a traumatic brain injury. Because of this, it has been difficult for scientists to determine the precise neurological causes for this relatively subtle change in speech. Some have hypothesized that foreign accent syndrome is simply a mild form of acquired apraxia of speech, while others define it as a distinct deficit. Foreign accent syndrome may accompany other forms of speech impairments, depending on the extent of brain damage. In about 70% of the reported cases, foreign accent syndrome has been accompanied by other language disabilities, including aphasia, dysarthria, and apraxia.[9] The syndrome has developed in individuals with selective damage to the basal ganglia (a subcortical region involved in speech production) or surrounding regions, or with damage to the pre-motor or motor regions of the left hemisphere of the cortex. Reduced cerebral blood flow localized to the left, medial frontal lobe (a region associated with language processing) has been noted in individuals who present with foreign accent syndrome. In one woman who developed foreign accent syndrome following a minor traumatic brain injury, researchers were unable to find any structural damage that might account for the abnormality, and a psychogenic rather than a neurogenic basis was suspected.

A Case Study of Foreign Accent Syndrome

One recent study reports a stroke patient whose only lingering deficits were foreign accent syndrome and slight weakness of the lips, which the patient noticed only when playing the trumpet. Analysis of his speech ruled out a diagnosis of either apraxia or dysarthria. Assessment using magnetic resonance imaging (MRI), a brain scanning technique, revealed that this patient had a small lesion in a region of the basal ganglia called the putamen. Surrounding regions of the basal ganglia were unharmed. The only other abnormality detected in this patient was increased activity in cortical regions involved with language. These cortical areas were intact and undamaged. The researchers hypothesized that the speaker's deficits were due to damage of speech centers located in the basal ganglia and that the increased activity in the cortex was a result of compensatory measures that the brain used to make up for deficits in the region damaged by the stroke. Damage to the putamen, therefore, is sufficient to produce the symptoms of foreign accent syndrome. Whether damage to this region is the only source of foreign accent syndrome is unclear, as other patients who have manifested the syndrome have suffered more extensive damage than this individual, and damage to other regions may have resulted in their syndromes.

Treatment of Foreign Accent Syndrome

There are no formal treatment strategies for foreign accent syndrome, though speech therapy may reduce the symptoms. The accent may remit fully in time without treatment. Interestingly, in patients who suffer both aphasia and foreign accent syndrome, the aphasia will remit spontaneously, while the accent will linger. Some patients have reported that their foreign accent syndrome actually aids them in coping with aphasia. Strangers assume that these individuals are speaking in a second language and are less judgmental than otherwise when the individuals have trouble finding words. In comparison to other language deficits, the social ramifications of persistent foreign accent syndrome are relatively inconsequential.

■ **Learn more about speech and language impairments resulting from brain damage** Search the Internet for *dysarthia*, *apraxia*, and *foreign accent syndrome*.

10 Disorders with a Speech/Language Component

Some neurological disorders that are not primary disorders of speech and language have a language impairment that accompanies them, most likely because the disruptions within the brain that underlie these disorders affect regions involved in the control of speech and language. Additionally, these disorders may disrupt thought processing, leading to atypical use of language. Among these disorders are Tourette syndrome, autism, and schizophrenia.

TOURETTE SYNDROME

Tourette syndrome (TS) is a disorder characterized by sudden, involuntary movements and vocal utterances called tics. The onset of TS is typically prior to 21 years of age, most frequently beginning by 6 years of age, with symptom severity peaking by 10 years of age. The severity of TS varies among individuals, depending on the frequency and complexity of the tics. Some individuals may experience tics only in specific settings, such as at home, school, or work. Symptoms may wax and wane over a course of weeks or months. Sometimes additional disorders accompany TS, including **obsessive-compulsive disorder** and attention deficit hyperactivity disorder. At its worst, TS interrupts a person's ability to engage in the normal activities of life.

Although the tics of TS are defined as involuntary, approximately 93% of those with Tourette syndrome describe an irresistible urge to move body parts or to form vocalizations.[10] This urge may be considered the involuntary part of a tic, and its execution a voluntary manner of dealing with this sensation. The motor tics characteristic of TS are typically rapid, jerky, and meaningless movements of body parts, including head, arm, or leg jerking, shoulder shrugging, grimacing, hopping, clapping, or touching the ground. In some individuals with TS, motor tics may include obscene gesturing. Vocal tics in TS often occur at the initiation of speech or at the beginning of new sentences. The speech patterns of those with TS may include altered volume, emphasis of particular words, slurred speech, or adoption of an accent. Vocal tics may consist of simple sounds, words, or phrases. In their simplest form, vocal tics may include coughing, barking, grunting, gurgling, hissing, whistling, or syllabic sounds such as "uh," "bu," or "eee." More complex vocal tics are repeated phrases such as "Oh boy," "You know," "All right," "Now you've said it," or "Shut up."

Vocal tics include speech called coprolalia, palilalia, and echolalia. **Coprolalia** is the expression of obscene, aggressive, or socially unacceptable words and phrases. This is perhaps one of the best-known vocal tics of TS, though coprolalia is actually one of the less common vocalizations, occurring in only a small percentage of those with the disorder. **Palilalia** is the repetition of one's own words. Those with TS may repeat their words three or more times, until the words sound "right" to them. **Echolalia** is the repetition of sounds, words, or phrases of others.

Causes of Tourette Syndrome

Disruptions in dopaminergic signaling in the brain are hypothesized to underlie the symptoms of TS. Among the earliest evidence implicating this neurotransmitter in TS were observations that drugs inhibiting dopaminergic neurotransmission were beneficial therapeutic agents for TS. These include haloperidol (also beneficial in minimizing stuttering but with severe side effects following long-term use) and newer antipsychotic medications that interfere with dopamine signaling. Brain imaging studies and postmortem examinations indicate disrupted dopaminergic signaling in the basal ganglia.

Imaging studies have detected various abnormalities in some individuals with TS compared to control subjects. Some studies show hyperactivity in the cortical regions controlling motor movement while others show abnormal activity in the basal ganglia, specifically in the striatum, the putamen, and the caudate nucleus. A pathway between the caudate nucleus and the motor cortex is important for coordination of movement. This pathway seems to be disrupted in many individuals with TS.

TS affects up to 1% of the population and is believed to have a genetic basis.[11] Genomic studies of those with TS have revealed abnormalities in portions of chromosomes 4, 5, 8, 11, and 17. Until recently, however, no specific genes contributing to TS had been identified within these chromosomal stretches. After analyzing an abnormal region within chromosome 13 of an adolescent boy afflicted with TS, scientists found a gene that may contribute to the development of the disorder in some individuals. This gene is named Slit and Trk-like family member 1 (SLITRK1). This gene is expressed highly in the brain, especially in the cortex and the basal ganglia. The protein this gene encodes is important for neuronal growth and dendritic branching. Neurons from mice with abnormal versions of this gene have stunted dendritic growth compared to neurons from normal animals. Future research may prove that mutations in SLITRK1 contribute to the development of TS. Unfortunately, this gene is not involved in all cases of TS, as mutations in this gene have been detected only in a small percentage of individuals with TS. Additional genetic mutations likely contribute to the disorder in the majority of individuals diagnosed with TS.

AUTISM

Public awareness of autism was raised by the film *Rain Man*, in which actor Dustin Hoffman portrayed an autistic man. Autism refers to a spectrum of developmental disorders characterized

The Importance of Inhibition

There are two major responses to neurotransmitters in the brain: excitatory and inhibitory. When excitatory neurotransmitters, such as glutamate or acetylcholine, are released into a synapse, they excite the downstream neuron and increase the likelihood of the generation of an action potential. This action potential allows the downstream neuron to send signals to additional neurons. When inhibitory neurotransmitters, such as gamma-aminobutyric acid (GABA), however, are released into a synapse, they make the downstream neuron less likely to fire action potentials. The brain requires a balance of excitation and inhibition in order for cells to communicate properly among themselves. Loss of GABA signaling may trigger an epileptic seizure.

The thalamus is an important relay center in the brain. Cells from this region form neural networks with higher cortical areas, and these connections, called thalamocortical connections, are important for regulating behavior. The cells in these networks often fire action potentials rhythmically in bursts of activity followed by periods of silence. GABA signaling contributes to the rhythmic activity of thalamocortical connections. This rhythmic activity is important in sleep-wake cycles and in motor control.

by social interaction deficits, language/communication impairments, and abnormal, stereotyped behavior patterns. Autistic children do not seek and develop a nurturing relationship with their parents, nor do they develop friendships. Instead, these children prefer to play alone inside their homes, often excessively interested in the parts or movement of objects. Autistic children develop routines and rituals, typically with no functional value, and are uncomfortable with change. New

Aberrant firing rhythms, called thalamocortical dysrhythmia, may underlie pathological states such as seizure, tinnitus, neurogenic pain, or Parkinson's disease. Stimulating the thalamus to induce changes in its firing rhythms can improve movement tremors.

Though not included in the list of thalamocortical dysrhythmias, patients with Tourette syndrome (TS) have abnormalities in GABA and in cortical inhibition compared to control subjects. Aberrant GABA signaling and neuronal network activity may contribute to this movement and speech disorder. Current research continues to explore the role of inhibition in coordinating the neural activity necessary for normal human behavior. Neurofeedback therapy involves rewarding patients when their brain, initially by chance, falls into a favorable firing state. The reward increases the probability that the brain will return to this state. Many disorders, including TS, have shown improvement with neurofeedback. Future research may reveal whether dysfunctional regulation of inhibitory signals contributes to TS or other disorders disturbing speech and language.

foods, toys, or clothing are disagreeable. Changes in routine are stressful. Autistic children may become distressed for no apparent reason and may even throw tantrums.

The language and communication component of autism is characterized by delayed development of spoken language with lack of alternative communication strategies in the absence of spoken language (such as gesturing). Autistic children make little or no eye contact and do not respond well to verbal communication, sometimes appearing deaf by their lack of response. Echolalia, also a symptom of TS, may be used instead of appropriate conversational responses. Autistic children may laugh inappropriately. They show limited ability to hold a conversation and do not appear to consider what other people think or understand. They are unreceptive to nonverbal communication such as tone of voice or body language. Autistic children do not engage in the make-believe or socially imitative play that other children exhibit. The extent of language development by age 7 is indicative of the severity of a child's autism, the symptoms of which will persist throughout life.

Autism may be accompanied by other features, including general intelligence deficits and epilepsy. Autistic children's IQs are often 70 or lower (average IQ is 100). Typically, scores on verbal tests are poorer than those based on motor or spatial skills. Some autistic children show unusual ability in selective skills, such as complex mathematics or music. Because of their other deficits, however, autistic children are typically unable to use these skills in a productive manner.

Incidence of Autism

Autism is relatively rare; incidence estimates range from 0.7 to 26 out of every 10,000 children.[12] Males are roughly 2 to 4 times more likely than females to be diagnosed with autism.[13] Symptoms usually appear around the age of 2.

Causes of Autism

The causes of autism are complex, resulting from seemingly many distinct conditions. Genetic factors are involved, and scientists suspect that multiple disrupted genes (hypothesized between 5 and 10) underlie this disorder. Autism may result in children with heritable metabolic disorders or fragile X syndrome (characterized by disruptions in the X chromosome that lead to cognitive impairment). Recently, scientists found that a gene involved in regulating cellular energy is disrupted in many individuals with autism. This gene, called SLC25A12, is involved in the production of adenosine triphosphate (ATP), which is broken down by cells to provide a source of energy needed to carry out cellular functions. Without the ability to properly form ATP, cells will function improperly. This gene alone does not cause autism, as variants of this gene are found in individuals that do not have autism. The presence of mutations in this gene, however, doubles an individual's risk of developing autism.[14] If additional, currently unknown genetic factors are present, mutations in this gene will likely contribute to the development of autism.

Brain imaging studies have revealed diverse abnormalities in the brains of autistic individuals compared to non-autistic controls. Heterogeneous differences in brain structure and function of those with autism suggest that many different causes could underlie this disorder. Abnormalities have been detected in the cerebellum (important for movement and for formation of procedural memory), the limbic system (in particular the hippocampus and the amygdala), and in cortical regions (both frontal and temporal lobes where some language processing occurs). These abnormalities include the overall volume of the tissue in these areas and in the morphology of individual cells. For example, reduced dendritic branching has been detected in limbic regions.

There is evidence that the activity of the neurotransmitter **serotonin** is disrupted in some individuals with autism, and one therapeutic strategy involves treatment with drugs that enhance the activity of serotonin in the brain.

Treatment of Autism

There is no cure for autism. In the absence of a cure, diverse forms of therapy are used to help manage the many symptoms of the disorder, from behavioral to social modification (Figure 10.1). The verbal deficits of autism may be improved with speech therapy. This therapy attempts to teach non-verbal children basic verbal use. In autistic children who speak, the main focus of therapy is to help children use language to interact with others in a meaningful way.

Medications may help to ameliorate some of the symptoms of the disorder. As introduced above, behavioral symptoms have been treated with drugs that interfere with the neurotransmitter serotonin, preventing it from being rapidly removed from the synaptic cleft and enhancing its activity in the brain. Other drugs have been used to treat the epileptic seizures that sometimes accompany autism. Additional medications can alleviate symptoms of anxiety, aggression, hyperactivity, or obsessive-compulsive behaviors.

SCHIZOPHRENIA

Schizophrenia is a mental disorder that involves delusions, hallucinations, and disorganized behavior and speech. In the 1991 film *The Fisher King*, actor Robin Williams portrays a man who exhibits symptoms of schizophrenia. As with autism, schizophrenia includes a spectrum of disorders that can be characterized by different subsets of symptoms in different individuals. Schizophrenia has been divided into five types: paranoid, disorganized, catatonic, undifferentiated, and residual. Paranoid

Figure 10.1 Therapy is an effective way to treat a number of speech and language impairments. In this photo, a therapist works with an autistic boy.

schizophrenia, representing approximately one-third of schizo-phrenic patients,[15] is characterized by auditory hallucinations or delusions involving persecution and/or grandiosity. This is often accompanied by abnormalities in mood, in which patients exhibit blunted emotional responses. Disorganized schizophre-nia involves both disordered behavior and speech along with inappropriate facial expressions or a lack of facial expression (inappropriate or flat affect). Disorganized schizophrenics often lose the ability to engage in the daily activities of life. Catatonic schizophrenia is characterized by movement disturbances; these patients may sit motionless for long periods or may exhibit extended, purposeless movements. Sometimes catatonic schizo-phrenics will imitate the movements of others. Undifferentiated and residual classifications are used for patients that do not fall into the first three categories and whose symptoms may not be ongoing.

Formal Thought Disorder

The language deficits of schizophrenia are mainly seen in individuals fitting the disorganized classification. These prominent language deficits are typically described as "formal thought disorder" (indicating a problem with the content of speech, rather than the speech itself), though some abnormalities in voice quality, articulation, grammar, and fluency may occur.

Word approximation, neologisms, and association chaining are all language deficits observed in schizophrenics. **Word approximation** is the use of words that only approximate the intended meaning. For instance, a schizophrenic may use the word "reflector" when he means to say "mirror," or "handshoe" when he means to say "glove." The use of word approximation suggests that schizophrenics may not have appropriate recall of all of the words in their vocabulary, as their vocabularies are often extensive and they know and understand the words that they sometimes approximate.

Neologisms are made-up words. Schizophrenics may insert made-up words into their conversation, typically using them in forms that follow standard syntax and grammar, such as using conventional endings for verb tense. For example, "I got angry when he twiggled me."

Association chaining occurs when schizophrenics get sidetracked in their language by words that may have alternate meanings. For example, "The pigs escaped from the pen. This pen has ink." Interestingly, when a word has two possible meanings, schizophrenics may interpret the word to mean the more common use, rather than determining its meaning by context. In the sentence, "Every Friday night they play bridge," a schizophrenic may interpret the word "bridge" to mean a structure that spans over water, in spite of the fact that the context of the sentence (the word "play") would indicate that "bridge" is a card game. Similarly, schizophrenics may also take idioms literally when it is possible to visualize them in a literal manner: "He kicked the bucket." When there is no clear literal meaning, however, schizophrenics are more likely to understand that these are merely figures of speech, as in the phrase, "She paid through the nose for that dress."

Incidence of Schizophrenia

Schizophrenia affects as much as 1% of the general population. There are genetic contributions to the development of the disorder, with first-degree relatives of schizophrenics having a 10% chance of developing the disorder and monozygotic twin siblings of schizophrenics having a 40 to 50% risk. Symptoms tend to manifest first between childhood (6 to 7 years of age) and adolescence, though some individuals do not exhibit symptoms until adulthood. A small portion of individuals have only one episode of symptoms or occasional episodes that do not interfere significantly with their ability to lead normal lives. Approximately 70% of those with schizophrenia, however, have great difficulty integrating into mainstream society, and few marry or have children.[16]

Causes of Schizophrenia

The psychiatrist Timothy Crow described schizophrenia as "the price *Homo sapiens* pays for language."[17] He suggests that the complex genetic advancements necessary for human language are vulnerable to error and that these genetic errors lead to the severe mental illness manifested in schizophrenia. Though the precise genetic basis of schizophrenia is unknown, scientists have identified abnormalities in chromosomes 2, 13,

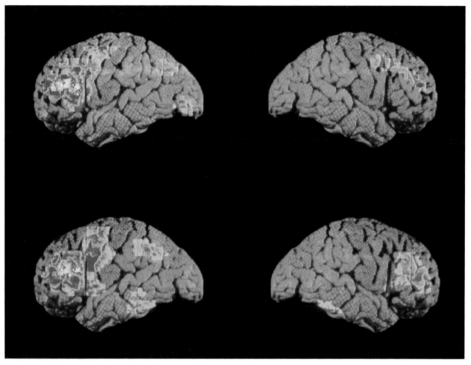

Figure 10.2 The bottom half of this photograph shows PET scans of a schizophrenic while speaking; the top half shows scans of a patient without schizophrenia. The brain of the person with schizophrenia has a slightly different pattern of activation.

and 15 that are common in people with the disorder. Specific abnormalities seem to run in individuals of similar ethnic background. Abnormalities in multiple genes likely contribute to the disorder.

Research has shown abnormalities in structure and function in multiple brain regions of schizophrenics (Figure 10.2). Not all schizophrenics, however, share the same abnormalities. Abnormalities noted in the schizophrenic brain include low activity in the prefrontal cortex, excessive levels of the neurotransmitter dopamine in the striatal region of the basal ganglia, enlarged **ventricles** (the cerebrospinal fluid–filled cavities in the interior of the brain), and decreased **gray matter** in regions of the brain, especially the frontal eye fields. The excessive amounts of dopamine, in particular, have been linked with the delusions and hallucinations that occur in some schizophrenics, since dopamine-blocking medications have improved these symptoms.

Treatment of Schizophrenia

The primary treatment for schizophrenia is medication, though alternative medicine and therapy are sometimes used. Antipsychotic medications that modulate dopaminergic signaling are the most common drugs prescribed for schizophrenic patients. As stated previously, these drugs have troubling side effects that inhibit their long-term use. Some patients do not respond to these treatments either. Approaches from alternative medicine are being investigated for their efficacy, including the use of ginkgo biloba (an Asian shrub) and vitamin therapy, including supplementation of folic acid, niacin, vitamin B_6, and vitamin C. Therapy typically includes vocational advising and job training; help with day-to-day tasks such as problem solving, money management skills, and use of public transportation; social skills training; behavioral therapy; and family counseling.

SUMMARY

The human brain shows an amazing capacity for language. Our language ability comes so easily that we often take this skill for granted. Children, within a matter of just 4 to 5 years, learn to use thousands of words in complex grammatical structures. This richness is unparalleled in other areas of learning; imagine if 5-year-old children could compose music or engineer technology in the way they create stories about the world around them. Yet the brain masters language alone at such a young age. Human language, in which words are arranged according to grammatical rules, is different than the communication of other species. Only those brain regions used to initiate speech are comparable to other species. By studying vocalization in these animals, we are learning important information about human speech that will one day aid in the treatment of speech disorders. Still, many of the brain regions utilized in language processing have no counterparts in the brains of other animals. This presents challenges for scientists interested in understanding how language works. The future will be an exciting time for language research as technology improves our ability to visualize the thinking brain as it coordinates language.

Beyond the brain's mechanism for speech and language, other fascinating aspects of language exist. Language is a crucial element of human society, facilitating cooperation among individuals and the advancement of science and culture. The impact of language in human thought and in human society is an additional topic of interest to scientists. What would our world be like without language? Has language helped to shape the development of the human mind? As you have read, these are questions that are difficult to answer. Scientists are compiling archaeological and anthropological data, along with fascinating case studies of individuals with language impairments, to help us understand the role of language in human history and in modern society. Clearly, the loss of language ability described in these final chapters illustrates the importance of language for humans. Because of this, scientists will continue to search for ways to better understand how language works and how it impacts the human condition.

Notes

1. Oliver Sacks, *Seeing Voices: A Journey into the World of the Deaf*. Berkeley, CA: University of California Press, 1989, p. 40.
2. MSN Encarta, "Cerebrum," *Brain*. Available online at http://encarta.msn.com/encyclopedia_761555359/Brain.html.
3. Oliver Sacks, *Seeing Voices: A Journey into the World of the Deaf*. Berkeley, CA: University of California Press, 1989, p. ix.
4. Edward Sapir, "The Status of Linguistics as a Science," *Culture, Language, and Personality: Selected Essays*, ed. David G. Mandelbaum. Berkeley, CA: University of California Press, 1970, p. 69.
5. Benjamin Whorf, *Language, Thought, and Reality: Selected Writings*. Cambridge, MA: MIT Press, 1978, p. 213.
6. Neil Gordon, "Stuttering: Incidence and Causes," *Developmental Medicine and Child Neurology* 44 (2002): 278–282.
7. Terese Finitzo and Frances Freeman, "Spasmodic Dysphonia, Whether and Where: Results of Seven Years of Research," *Journal of Speech and Hearing Research* 32 (1983): 541–555.
8. National Institute on Deafness and Other Communication Disorders, "Aphasia," *Aphasia*. Available online at http://www.nidcd.nih.gov/health/voice/aphasia.asp.
9. John Van Borsel, Leen Janssens, and Patrick Santens, "Foreign Accent Syndrome: An Organic Disorder?" *Journal of Communication Disorders* 38 (2005): 421–429.
10. J.R. Adams, A.R. Troiano, and D.B. Clane. "Functional Imaging in Tourette's Syndrome," *Journal of Neural Transmission* 111 (2004): 1495–1506.
11. Tourette Syndrome Association, Inc., "Fact Sheet," *Medical and Treatment*. Available online at http://www.tsa-usa.org.
12. Medical Journal of Australia, "Language Disorders and Autism," *MJA Practice Essentia–Pediatrics*. Available online at http://www.mja.com.au/public/issues/182_07_040405/wra10330_fm.html.
13. Merck Manuals Online Medical Library, "Autism," *Autism: Mental Health Disorders: Merck Manual Home Edition*. Available online at http://www.merck.com/mmhe/sec23/ch286/ch286b.html.
14. Nicolas Ramoz, et al., "Linkage and Association of the Mitochondrial Aspartate/Glutamate Carrier SLC25A12 Gene with Autism," *American Journal of Psychiatry* 161 (2004): 662–669.
15. Encyclopedia of Mental Disorders, "Schizophrenia," *Schizophrenia—Definition, Description, Causes and Symptoms, Demographics, Diagnosis, Treatments, Prognosis, Prevention*. Available online at http://www.

minddisorders.com/Py-Z/
Schizophrenia.html.

16. Ibid.

17. Timothy Crow, "Is Schizophrenia
the Price that *Homo Sapiens* Pays
for Language?" *Schizophrenia
Research* 28 (1997): 127.

Glossary

Angular gyrus A posterior portion of the parietal lobe.

Anomia The inability to name objects or recognize written or spoken names of objects.

Aphasia Partial or total loss of the ability to articulate or comprehend language.

Apraxia A motor disorder disrupting the coordination of speech.

Arcuate fasciculus A curved bundle of fibers connecting Broca's area and Wernicke's area.

Association chaining A change in the flow of language prompted by words that have multiple meaning.

Auditory association cortex A region of the cerebral cortex adjacent to the auditory cortex that is involved in the analysis of auditory input.

Auditory cortex A region in the cerebral cortex that receives auditory input.

Axon Long portion of nerve cells that carry signals away from the cell body.

Basal ganglia A group of neurons located at the base of the cerebral hemispheres that is involved in motor function and learning.

Botulinum toxin A substance produced by the bacterium *Clostridium botulinum* that causes muscle paralysis.

Brain stem A region of the brain, including the medulla oblongata, pons, and midbrain, that connects the spinal cord to the forebrain.

Broca's area A region of the frontal lobe located near the motor cortex, involved in speech production.

Caudate nucleus A cluster of cells involved in motor control that is a component of the basal ganglia, located along the lateral ventricle and curving toward the temporal lobes.

Cerebellum A region of the brain that lies posterior to the medulla oblongata and pons, beneath the occipital lobes, which is involved in coordinating voluntary muscle movement and maintaining posture and balance.

Cerebral cortex The outermost layer of gray matter in the brain, responsible for higher brain functions such as reason and memory.

Cingulate gyrus A region of the brain involved in coordinating sensory input with emotions.

Coprolalia Expression of obscene, aggressive, or socially unacceptable words and phrases.

Cranial nerves A group of nerves that transmit and/or receive sensory, motor, or parasympathetic information to the face and neck.

Critical period A developmental time frame during which a skill is most readily acquired.

Dendrites Branched portions of nerve cells that carry incoming electrical signals to the cell body.

Dopamine A neurotransmitter important for normal brain function, involved in disorders such as Parkinson's disease and schizophrenia.

Dysarthria Difficulty in articulating speech due to weakening or dysfunction of the muscles of the mouth, face, and/or respiratory system.

Echolalia Repetition of sounds, words, or phrases of others.

First language acquisition The development of a native language in young children.

Foreign accent syndrome A rare speech disorder in which individuals speak their native language as if with a foreign accent; typically the result of brain injury.

Frontal lobe A lobe of the cerebral cortex, important for problem solving and working memory.

Functional magnetic resonance imaging (fMRI) A type of magnetic resonance imaging that detects changes in blood flow in active regions of the brain.

Gray matter Nerve cell bodies and dendrites.

Language A systematic form of spoken, written, or signed communication that follows rules governing word combination.

Magnetoencephalography Imaging technique that measures magnetic fields created by the brain.

Medulla oblongata The lowest portion of the brain leading into the spinal cord, which is responsible for respiration and other functions necessary for survival.

Metalinguistic Referring to language that is used to describe or analyze language.

Midbrain A subdivision of the brain stem, within which are two regions called the periaqueductal gray (PEG) and the parabrachial tegmentum.

Motor association cortex A region of the cerebral cortex that coordinates movements, including lip movements required for speech.

Motor cortex A region of the cerebral cortex that governs nerve impulses to the muscles.

Myelin A fatty substance that insulates nerve fibers and preserves the electrical signal as it travels.

Myelination Development of a sheath of myelin around a nerve fiber.

Nativist One who believes that language is an innate ability rather than a learned skill.

Neocortex The portion of the cerebral cortex that houses the most recently evolved regions of the brain.

Neologisms Made-up words.

Neuron Cell of the nervous system specialized to conduct electrical impulses; typically includes a cell body, an axon, and branches of dendrites.

Neurotransmitters Chemicals within the nervous system that are released into synapses from the axon terminals of neurons following generation of an action potential.

Nucleus ambiguous A cluster of neurons located in the medulla that governs activity of the ninth and tenth cranial nerves.

Obsessive-compulsive disorder A behavioral disorder in which individuals experience recurring thoughts that they are unable to dismiss and perform repetitive actions in an effort to minimize the thoughts.

Occipital lobe A posterior lobe of the cerebral cortex that houses the brain's visual centers.

Palilalia Repetition of one's own words.

Parabrachial tegmentum A region of the midbrain adjacent to the periaqueductal gray.

Parietal lobe A region of the cerebral cortex that lies beneath the parietal bones.

Periaqueductal gray A region of the midbrain.

Peripheral nervous system Nerves that lie outside of the central nervous system, including the cranial and spinal nerves, and the sympathetic and parasympathetic nervous system.

Phoneme The smallest phonetic units of language that convey meaning, such as "r" or "b" in the English words "red" and "bed."

Plasticity The ability of the brain to form new neural connections.

Positron emission tomography (PET) A computer-generated image of biological activity in the body that is captured following the release of positrons from an introduced radioactive substance.

Second language acquisition The process of learning a second language after the critical period for first language acquisition has passed.

Serotonin A neurotransmitter formed from the amino acid tryptophan.

Spasmodic dysphonia A disorder characterized by abnormal muscle tone in the vocal folds, which results in strained, soft, or breathy speech.

Stroke Blockage or rupture of a blood vessel in or leading to the brain, resulting in loss of function.

Stuttering A speech disorder characterized by the repetition or prolongation of sounds; also called stammering.

Synapse The space between the terminal of one neuron's axon and the downstream neuron across which a neurotransmitter is released. It also includes the pre- and post-synaptic membranes.

Syntax Rules governing the formation of phrases or sentences in a language.

Tardive dyskinesia A nervous system disorder characterized by involuntary movement of the face, tongue, jaws, limbs, and trunk that is often a side effect of long-term use of antipsychotic drugs.

Temporal lobe A region of the brain located in the lower, lateral portion of the cerebral cortex that houses hearing and language centers of the human brain.

Thalamus A region of the brain that relays sensory input to the cerebral cortex.

Ventricles Fluid-filled, interconnected cavities in the brain.

Visual cortex Region of the brain activated following visual stimulation.

Wada test A neurological experiment in which the drug sodium amytal is used to silence activity in one hemisphere of the brain.

Wernicke's area A region of the human brain located in the temporal lobe that is important for language comprehension.

Word approximation Imprecise use of words that are close in meaning to the intended word.

Bibliography

Abelson, Jesse, et al. "Sequence Variants in *SLITRK1* are Associated with Tourette's Syndrome." *Science* 310 (2005): 317–320.

Adams, J., A. Troiano, and D.B. Calne. "Functional Imaging in Tourette's Syndrome." *Journal of Neural Transmission* 111 (2004): 1495–1506.

American College of Radiology, Radiological Society of North America. "Positron Emission Tomography (PET Imaging)." Available online at http://www.radiologyinfo.org/content/peto-mography.htm#Description.

Baylor College of Medicine. "Songbird Offers Clues to Help Stutterers." *Songbird*. Available online at http://www.bcm.edu/pa/songbird.htm.

Bliznikas, Darius. "Spasmodic Dysphonia." WebMD eMedicine. Available online at http://www.emedicine.com/ent/byname/spas-modic-dysphonia.htm.

Brown, Donald. *Human Universals.* New York: McGraw-Hill, Inc., 1991.

Brown, T., J. Sambrooks, and M. MacCulloch. "Auditory Thresholds and the Effect of Reduced Auditory Feedback on Stuttering." *Acta Psychiatrica Scandinavica* 51 (1975): 297–311.

Calvin, William. *A Brief History of the Mind.* New York: Oxford University Press, Inc., 2004.

Caplan, David. "Language and the Brain." *Language and the Brain.* Available online at http://www.med.harvard.edu/publications/On_The_Brain/Volume4/Number4/F95Lang.html.

Chandler, Daniel. "The Sapir-Whorf Hypothesis." Available online at http://www.aber.ac.uk/media/Documents/short/whorf.html.

Chomsky, Noam. *Acquisition of Syntax in Children from 5–10.* Cambridge, MA: MIT Press, 1969.

Chomsky, Noam. *Powers and Prospects: Reflections on Human Nature and the Social Order.* Boston: South End Press, 1996.

Covington, Michael, et al. "Schizophrenia and the Structure of Language: The Linguist's View." *Schizophrenia Research* 77 (2005): 85–98.

Crow, Timothy. "Schizophrenia as the Price that *Homo Sapiens* Pays for Language: A Resolution of the Central Paradox in the Origin of the Species." *Brain Research Reviews* 31 (2000): 118–129.

Culham, Jody. "Basics of MRI and fMRI." *fMRI for Newbies.* Available online at http://www.ssc.uwo.ca/psychology/culhamlab/Jody_web/fmri4newbies.htm.

Doupe, Allison, Michele Solis, Rhea Kimpo, and Charlotte Bottiger. "Cellular, Circuit, and Synaptic Mechanisms in Song Learning." *Annals of the New York Academy of Sciences* 1016 (2004): 495–523.

Doupe, Allison, and Patricia Kuhl. "Birdsong and Human Speech: Common Themes and Mechanisms." *Annual Review of Neuroscience* 22 (1999): 567–631.

Edelson, Meredyth Goldberg. "Autism-related Disorders in DSM-IV." *Center for the Study of Autism.* Available online at http://www.autism.org/dsm.html.

Elbert, Thomas, and Brigitte Rockstroh. "Reorganization of Human Cerebral Cortex: The Range of Changes Following Use and Injury." *Neuroscientist* 10 (2004): 129-141.

Encyclopedia of Mental Disorders. "Schizophrenia," *Schizophrenia – Definition, Description, Causes and Symptoms, Demographics, Diagnosis, Treatments, Prognosis, Prevention.* Available online at http://www.minddisorders.com/Py-Z/Schizophrenia.html.

Fridriksson, Julius, et al. "Brain Damage and Cortical Compensation in Foreign Accent Syndrome." *Neurocase* 11 (2005): 319–324.

Gordon, Neil. "The Acquisition of a Second Language." *European Journal of Paediatric Neurology* 4 (2000): 3–7.

Gordon, Peter. "Level Ordering in Lexical Development." *Cognition* 21 (1985): 73–93.

Gordon, Peter. "The Neurology of Sign Language." *Brain and Development* 26 (2004): 146–150.

Hespos, Susan. "Language: Life Without Numbers." *Current Biology* 14 (2004): R927–9F28.

Hespos, Susan, and Elizabeth Spelke. "Conceptual Precursors to Language." *Nature* 430 (2004): 453–456.

Knezek, Malia. "Nature vs. Nurture: The Miracle of Language." *Psychology of Language*. Available online at http://www.duke.edu/~pk10/language/psych.htm.

Lippert-Gruener, M., U. Weinert, T. Greisbach, and C. Wedekind. "Foreign Accent Syndrome Following Traumatic Brain Injury." *Brain Injury* 19 (2005): 955–958.

Maguire, Gerald, Glyndon Riley, and Benjamin Yu. "A Neurological Basis for Stuttering?" *Lancet Neurology* 1(2002): 407.

McCaffrey, Patrick. "Neuroanatomy of Speech, Swallowing and Language." *Upper Neuronal Tracts*. Available online at http://www.csuchico.edu/~pmccaff/syllabi/CMSD%20320/362unit9.html.

National Institute on Deafness and Other Communication Disorders. "Voice, Speech, and Language." Available online at http://www.nidcd.nih.gov/health/voice.

Nishitani, Nobuyuki, Martin Schürmann, Katrin Amunts, and Riitta Hari. "Broca's Region: From Action to Language." *Physiology* 20 (2005): 60–69.

Pinker, Steven. *How the Mind Works*. New York: W.W. Norton, 1997.

Pinker, Steven. *The Language Instinct*. New York: William Morrow and Co., Inc., 1994.

Ratey, John. *A User's Guide to the Brain*. New York: Vintage Books, 2001.

Sakai, Kuniyoshi. "Language Acquisition and Brain Development." *Science* 310 (2005): 815-819.

Sapir, Edward. *Language: An Introduction to the Study of Speech*. New York: Harcourt, 1949.

Schaefer, Steven. "Neuropathology of Spasmodic Dysphonia." *Laryngoscope* 93 (1983): 1183–1204.

Tuchman, Roberto. "Autism." *Neurologic Clinics* 21 (2003): 915–932.

Van Borsel, John, Leen Janssens, and Patrick Santens. "Foreign Accent Syndrome: An Organic Disorder?" *Journal of Communication Disorders* 38 (2005): 421–429.

Ward, Andrew. "Genie: A Modern-day Wild Child." FeralChildren. com. Available online at http://www.feralchildren.com/en/show-child.php?ch=genie.

Wray, John, Natalie Silove, and Helen Knott. "Language Disorders and Autism." *Medical Journal of Australia* 182 (2005): 354–360.

Further Reading

Brown, Donald. *Human Universals.* New York: McGraw-Hill, Inc., 1991.

Calvin, William. *A Brief History of the Mind.* New York: Oxford University Press, Inc., 2004.

Calvin, William, and Derek Bickerton. *Lingua ex Machina: Reconciling Darwin and Chomsky with the Human Brain.* Cambridge, MA: MIT Press, 2000.

Chomsky, Noam. *Powers and Prospects: Reflections on Human Nature and the Social Order.* Boston: South End Press, 1996.

Deacon, Terrence. *The Symbolic Species: The Co-Evolution of Language and the Brain.* New York: W.W. Norton, 1997.

Dunbar, Robin. *Grooming, Gossip, and the Evolution of Language.* Cambridge, MA: Harvard University Press, 1996.

Pinker, Steven. *How the Mind Works.* New York: W.W. Norton, 1997.

Pinker, Steven. *The Language Instinct.* New York: William Morrow and Co., Inc., 1994.

Ratey, John. *A User's Guide to the Brain.* New York: Vintage Books, 2001.

Sacks, Oliver. *Seeing Voices: A Journey into the World of the Deaf.* Berkeley, CA: University of California Press, 1989.

Web Sites

National Institute on Deafness and Other Communication Disorders
http://www.nidcd.nih.gov

Neuroscience for Kids
http://staff.washington.edu/chudler/lang.html

Primate Use of Language
http://www.pigeon.psy.tufts.edu/psych26/language.htm

Speech and the Brain
http://www.ship.edu/~cgboeree/speechbrain.html

Picture Credits

2: Steven People
4: Infobase Publishing
7: Infobase Publishing
12: Infobase Publishing
17: Associated Press, AP
28: Infobase Publishing
30: WDCN/Univ. College London/ Photo Researchers, Inc.
34: Infobase Publishing
38: Lawrence Migdale/Photo Researchers, Inc.
43: Infobase Publishing
45: Infobase Publishing
50: Infobase Publishing
53: Lawrence Migdale/Photo Researchers, Inc.
57: Damien Lovegrove/Photo Researchers, Inc.
74: Prof. K. Seddon & Dr. T. Evans, QUB/Photo Researchers, Inc.
76: CNRI/Photo Researchers, Inc.
83: Zephyr/Photo Researchers, Inc.
87: Hattie Young/Photo Researchers, Inc.
99: Will & Deni McIntyre/Photo Researchers, Inc.
102: Wellcome/Photo Researchers, Inc.

Index

abstract ideas, expression of, 23–24
acetylcholine, 94
acquisition of language, 11–12, 56–60. *See also* language development
age, in language acquisition. *See also* critical period
  critical period and, 5–9, 47
  first language, 5–6
  second languages, 11–12, 57–58, 59
akinetic mutism, 44
ambiguity, 19–20
angular gyrus, 35
animals
  language comprehension by, 40
  as models for human diseases, 40–41
  vocalization by, 40–42, 47, 104
anomia, 81
aphasia, 80–83
apraxia, 85–88
arcuate fasciculus, 35, 48
association chaining, 100–101
atherosclerosis, 84
auditory association cortex, 34–35
auditory cortex, 34–35, 48
auditory feedback, in stuttering, 72, 75
autism, 94–98
axons, 27

babbling, 22
babies
  brain development in, 9–11
  language development in, 3–5
  spatial assessment in, 65–66
basal ganglia, 44, 45–46, 89
biological determinism, 15
blind persons, language processing in, 37–38
Boas, Franz, 62
botulinum toxin, for spasmodic dysphonia, 79
braille, learning of, 37–38
brain. *See also* Brain regions
  early development of, 4, 9–13

  hemispheres of, 6–7, 31–32
  language centers of, 26–32, 37–38
  language in shaping of, 58–59
  lobes of, 27
  plasticity of, 37–39
  relay of information in, 48
  techniques for study of, 1–2, 10–11
brain damage
  aphasia and, 80–83
  apraxia and, 85–88
  dysarthria and, 85
  foreign accent syndrome and, 88–90
  in localization of brain function, 26, 28–31
  sign language and, 52–53, 55–56
  speech loss and, 29–31
brain function
  animal models for study of, 40–42, 47
  localization of, 26, 28–32
  in schizophrenia, 102–103
brain imaging techniques, 2, 10–11
brain regions
  individual variability in, 36
  language centers, 26–32, 37–38
  in language production, 32–35, 48
  sign language and, 53–56
  in vocalization production, 42–46
brain stem, 42
Broca's aphasia, 81
Broca's area, 29–30, 37, 48, 54–55
Brown, Donald, 20

catatonic schizophrenia, 99
categorical relationships, recognition of by infants, 65–66
caudate nucleus, 46
cerebellum, 46
cerebral cortex, 27
children
  critical period in, 5–9, 47
  early brain development in, 9–11

About the Author

Amanda A. Sleeper, Ph.D., began her academic training at Hollins College, where she received her B.A. in psychology and Spanish literature. She expanded her interest in the brain and behavior at Worcester Polytechnic Institute, where she earned an M.S. in biology studying possible therapeutic agents for the treatment of ischemic stroke. She then earned a Ph.D. from Yale University studying neurobiology, where she was awarded the Scottish Rite Foundation Schizophrenia Fellowship for dissertation research. Her work focuses primarily on the regulation of calcium in the hippocampus, a region important for semantic memory processing. Her research interests include the pathophysiology of the aging brain. She has published in the *Journal of Neuroscience* and has additional publications in progress. She frequently presents data at the Society for Neuroscience annual meetings. The recipient of Worcester Polytechnic Institute Board of Trustee's Outstanding Teaching Award and a fellow of Yale University's Graduate Teaching Center, she has worked to enhance science education by offering seminars on effective teaching skills in science.

About the Editor

Eric H. Chudler, Ph.D., is a research associate professor in the University of Washington Department of Bioengineering and director of education and outreach at University of Washington Engineered Biomaterials. Dr. Chudler's research interests focus on how areas of the central nervous system (cerebral cortex and basal ganglia) process information related to pain. He has also worked with other neuroscientists and teachers to develop educational materials to help students learn about the brain.